STAND BY TO BEACH!

Sail on, nor fear to breast the sea!
Our hearts, our hopes are all with thee.

—LONGFELLOW.

OTHER BOOKS BY
GORDON HOLMAN

COMMANDO ATTACK

" A most interesting book written by a man who can write and has been on more than one of the famous raids already made by the Commandos, including the raid on St. Nazaire of which he gives a very graphic account."
—*The Times Literary Supplement.*

THE LITTLE SHIPS

" A first rate account of how this gallant force came into being. . . . As surely as Drake's little ships held off the Armada, it was these little ships who held the channel for us after Dunkirk."
—HOWARD SPRING, *The Sunday Graphic.*

THE FIRST FOOTHOLD GAINED!

(Royal Canadian Navy Photograph)

STAND BY TO BEACH !

BY

GORDON HOLMAN

London : HODDER & STOUGHTON Limited

First printed, December, 1944

Made and Printed in Great Britain for Hodder & Stoughton, Limited, London,
by Wyman & Sons Limited, London, Reading and Fakenham

CONTENTS

ILLUSTRATIONS

6

I

TURN OF THE TIDE

Here stands England's
  Rock-fast base,
Shell-white concrete deeply grounded—
  Freedom hath her
  Rallying-place
In mid-ocean founded. . . .

HENRIK WERGELAND (translated).

I

TURN OF THE TIDE

" UNDER the command of General Eisenhower, Allied naval forces, supported by strong air forces, began landing Allied armies this morning on the northern coast of France." This was the announcement contained in Communiqué No. 1, issued at 9.30 a.m. on June 6th, 1944, from Supreme Headquarters, Allied Expeditionary Force.

It told the world that D Day had arrived ; that all the months, even years, of careful planning were about to reach fruition. Indeed, events had already taken place at that hour which crowned with glorious success some of the most vital plans made for that historic day.

On a June day four years earlier I stood on the south coast of England and heard the Army Commander of the area say, as he looked across the Channel, " And one day we shall go back." It was General Montgomery. I had last seen that slight figure in battle-dress in the region of Louvain, in Belgium. Then disaster had befallen the French army and only an indomitable fighting spirit had saved the British Expeditionary Force from a similar fate.

Through Dunkirk they returned to England. They came, as has been so often told, in every type of vessel. Many of them, tired to the point of stupification, would not have known where they were if they had not come by sea.

Two artillerymen, I remember, dragging themselves on to a jetty at Dover under the weight of the breach of a gun, and asking, with heads sagging on their chests, " Is this England, chum ? "

When they were assured that they were home they dropped the all-important piece of gun mechanism, which, if they had been capable of thinking, they might have dropped hours earlier in the sea.

It took a Churchill or a Montgomery to look forward with steadfast eyes from that June to the June of 1944. But where such great men led many were prepared to follow. While we waited for invasion, while the Battle of Britain raged in the skies, through the long nights of blitz terror, and in the face of the U-boat threat of starvation, Britain looked forward.

With aid coming in an ever-growing volume from the Dominions and Colonies, the Allies and, most of all, the United States of America, faint and far-distant hopes grew into strong and urgent desires, capable of accomplishment. Men—and women—of many nations waited impatiently for the hour to strike when we should go by assault through the front door of Europe to smash Nazi Germany.

But the assault could only be made by sea, and the sea, which had saved Britain and preserved freedom in the world, now demanded from us the most thorough and far-reaching preparations for invasion ever known. Only by making these could we be sure of success—and success at a not unreasonable price.

In the pre-war years foresight was lacking in many directions, but first the sense of danger and then the sharp reality of danger, led to cool, long-sighted thinking on behalf of the country.

One would almost say that it was second sight that led to the building of the first landing craft months before the withdrawal of the B.E.F. from France.

The first L.C.A. (Landing Craft, Assault), built as part of our immediate pre-war naval construction programme, was running its trials on the Clyde in the month before war broke out in 1939. It was not much larger than a good-sized boat and twenty of them could have been carried in the craft that were to follow, but it was proof enough that the Navy was concerned with both the design and production of such vessels.

It was not the first time that they had had to produce craft of special design for landing purposes. Gallipoli and Mesopotamia in the war of 1914–18 had called for vessels capable of unloading troops and stores rapidly at points where ordinary ships would be of little use.

The vessel which might be regarded as the prototype of the huge family of flat-bottomed landing craft which made the 1944 invasion of Europe possible, is the X Lighter which was designed for use in the rivers of Mesopotamia in the last war. The problem was the same in those days as now and the " Mespot lighter " met it in the same way. Built of steel, it had a double ramp which enabled men, vehicles and even horses to land over the bows.

There are still many who went through the Gallipoli campaign who will recall, perhaps with mixed feelings, the *River Clyde*. Specially adapted for beach landings, she had openings cut in her bows. The watertight doors which covered these also gave protection to the troops from fire coming from the shore.

It is not generally known that at the end of the last war the Royal Navy had set about producing what, in those days, must have been regarded as the last word in landing craft. Known as an M.L.C. (Motor Landing Craft), it could carry a load of ten tons and was itself capable of being carried in a ship. Strangely enough, it was also one of the forerunners of what is now heralded as the most modern form of propulsion, jet propulsion. Unlike the ill-famed robot planes or the jet-propelled fighter aircraft of to-day, the jet-landing craft was very slow. Actually it was not ready for service until after the Armistice was signed.

If anyone remembered landing craft in the twenty year's gap between 1918 and 1938 it was probably with a smile at the very idea of their freakishness.

There were rude lessons to be learned, however, even before the days of Dunkirk. Building of small landing craft had gone ahead in a limited way after the outbreak of war in September, 1939, but those who produced the vessels little thought that they would be used in the early spring of 1940 to evacuate British soldiers from beaches in Norway. That, in fact, is the duty they first engaged upon.

Again, at Dunkirk, they went for purposes of evacuation, and the time when they would be used, as intended, for invasion seemed further away than ever.

After that the demands on the British shipbuilding industry were overwhelming in every direction, and it appeared to be out of the question to consider devoting any man-hours to the production of landing craft for the distant days when we would again take the offensive.

But attack is the best form of defence, and provision *had* to be made for the day when we attacked. To meet this need the Admiralty set about organising production in branches of British industry which had never before had any association with ships or the sea. They went to engineering firms, furniture and carpentry concerns, locomotive and railroad production shops, constructional and bridge-building firms and even small wayside garage businesses.

In effect they said, " If you can produce in metal or wood, go ahead and produce for us. We will fit you as a unit, large or small, into the scheme of production, and you will be doing a vital job."

Many of the workmen, and women, who engaged in this vast boat and ship-building programme in its early stages must have wondered when and how the results of their labours would be put to use. It was not easy to visualise June 6th, 1944, during the dark days of 1940 and 1941.

In parts of the country miles away from the sea work went on. By prefabrication methods boats were built in various sections which were only assembled when the parts came together after being transported by road and rail to a point on the coast. It is no exaggeration to say that Britain's contribution to the great landing-craft fleet which operated in the Mediterranean and across the Channel on D Day, and subsequently, came from factories, workshops and sheds spread all over the country.

Some of the bigger firms to take up this work found it necessary to set up shipbuilding yards. It was essential to have proper launching facilities for the larger types of tank-landing vessels. Well-known constructional firms often prefabricated the whole of the craft and then conveyed the parts for assembly at the launching point.

Neither was there a drain upon the Navy in regard to the delivery of these vessels to whatever base they might be sent. Yachtsmen and others, too old for service at sea, volunteered to act as ferry crews. Many men, no longer young, spent all the time they could possibly spare from their businesses doing this very useful service.

As more and more types of craft were produced, the "secret list" grew, and it was interesting and amusing to see the amazed looks with which some of the vessels were greeted when they were first seen in harbour or at sea by sailors in more orthodox ships.

It was in a North of England port that I first saw one of the large L.C.T.'s. (Landing Craft, Tanks). It was heading out of a basin into the main stream as the old coastal vessel, in which I was a passenger, attempted to enter. The skipper saw the curious up-sweep of the bows of the flat-bottomed craft as she began to emerge, and rang his engines to slow. His intention, obviously, was to slip gently round the stern of the other vessel without losing way on his own ship.

To his consternation the low, straight sides of the landing craft continued to emerge long after he had anticipated seeing the stern of the ship. Only after he had been forced to ring a hasty "Full Astern" to the engine-room did the bridge of the landing craft come into view. As it went by, with half a dozen of the crew standing to attention on the abbreviated forecastle, he looked at the new and strange craft with a highly critical, almost disapproving, eye and grunted, "They'll break in half if they made 'em any longer."

By the end of 1940 the first of the ocean-going landing craft were running their trials. There was still little to indicate where these vessels would be used, but we were getting ready.

The vessels to undergo their trials during the short days of that winter, when Britain fought with her back to the wall, were the first L.C.T.'s (Landing Craft, Tanks). As the name implies, they were designed to carry tanks—tanks still only in the process of production—to our future battle fronts. Much later it was to be found that they could carry a lot besides tanks and be of the greatest value to an army overseas long after most of the tanks had passed on into the main battle areas.

Although various types of L.C.T. have been evolved since those early days, this may be taken as a fair description of an L.C.T. : About two hundred feet long and a little more than thirty feet wide, it has a displacement of about 350 gross tons. Nearly all the weight is aft, and this helps to trim the vessel the right way for landing purposes. A large ramp, set at an angle of around 45 degrees, forms the squared-off bows, and where the lower part of the ramp enters the water the craft draws no more than three feet. The whole of the flat bottom of the vessel slopes gently until, in the stern, she draws seven feet. The sloping of the keel is intentional in order to give the craft an easy run up on the sandy beaches. The ramp in the bows is hinged at the bottom and can be lowered quickly by hand or power-driven winches. When it is down it provides a runway on to the beaches for the vehicles carried in the craft. It is lightly built (the plates are three-eighths of an inch thick) because weight would carry the vessel down too low in the water. Two-thirds of the space is available for tanks, which are lashed to the metal decks to prevent them from moving while aboard. The craft is powered by two 500 h.p. Diesel engines. The living quarters of the crew are right aft and can only be described as cramped. The bridge rises up three or four yards from the stern and the bridge fittings are conveniently arranged.

The L.C.T. has a crew of two officers and ten petty officers and ratings. Although they have to live very much on top of each other, there is the usual standard of naval discipline to be observed, and there is no doubt that, when the occasion demands it, landing craft personnel can be as smart in their turn-out as the best of them.

As in all small ships, there is a fine comradeship, added to, no doubt, in this case by the fact that almost invariably the men are " hostilities only " ratings and the officers have earned their promotion after serving on the lower deck.

These were the craft, then, that began to appear in certain British harbours and which in due course were to be followed by a much greater flow of specialised landing vessels from the yards and factories of the United States.

And all the time that these were building, much smaller landing craft, L.C.A.'s (Landing Craft, Assault) and L.C.S.'s (Landing Craft, Support) were being turned out. They were designed to be carried in a parent ship and were the boats of the Commandos on their famous early raids.

I first saw them go into action on Boxing Day morning, 1941, when the raid was carried out on the German observation posts, signal points and controls in the Lofoten islands, fifty or sixty miles from the Norwegian mainland in the far north. The flat-bottomed assault craft were carried like ships' boats, slung either side of the upper deck.

Their task was to take the Special Service troops ashore, possibly under fire. The Commando men took their places in the bottom of the craft, sitting in four rows, before they were lowered into the water. A tiny box-like " bridge " was occupied by the naval coxswain responsible for taking the boat ashore. The rest of the naval crew consisted of two men—one seaman and the rating in charge of the motor.

These craft looked very small indeed as they slipped away from the mother ship and headed towards the shore in the dull arctic twilight. They were followed by the L.C.S.'s, which are of an entirely different design, but are certainly no larger. The one I was in mounted a machine-gun which was to answer any fire from the shore which appeared to be holding up the assault troops. Very often the support craft have apparatus for making smoke which is used to cover the withdrawal of the raiding party. Later, too, they were given weapons to engage any enemy dive-bombers which might attempt to interfere.

From the time America entered the war there came a rapid acceleration in the production of all types of landing craft. At the same time it became apparent that large numbers of specially trained officers and men would be required to man them. Naval establishments were turned over to this purpose and the landing craft fleet really came into being.

It was necessary that every man in these flotillas of landing craft should be so expert in his task that not a moment would be wasted when they ran up on to the shore with tanks, guns and troops engaged in the assault. A little uncertainty or indecision might mean the wiping out of all those in the craft, and consequently a serious gap in the line of attack.

Officers and crews were fully aware of the responsibilities on their shoulders, and the army learned that they could rely absolutely on the determination and skill of the sailors handling the craft. It was not resignation, but genuine confidence that sounded in the voice of a soldier who said in my hearing on one occasion, " If the Navy cannot get us there, nobody can."

There were many exercises in which the landing craft and the army linked hands. They were carried out under the most realistic conditions. Long before any of the big tank landing vessels had been in action I saw them come in under cover of darkness near Selsey Bill. It was in the early hours of the morning, and they had to find a very limited space on the beach, with the knowledge that our own protective minefields were close at hand. It was not a particularly easy beach, either to approach or to get clear of on the landward side. Searchlights were used by the defenders, and these must have completely dazzled the tank drivers as they rumbled their vehicles forward over the suddenly lowered ramps of the L.C.T.'s. But the attack was carried through with considerable determination. The landing craft were set straight at the beach and came up with a jerk when they ran ashore. The tanks took to the water at once, although it was certainly deeper at many points than the tank drivers were called upon to face when we eventually stormed over the Normandy beaches.

The final testing came in the landing and re-embarkation of our forces at Dieppe. As for everyone else, it was an occasion which proved a very hard test indeed for the new branch of the Navy. They came through with flying colours. I believe it is true that although many of the landings were made in the face of heavy fire from the shore, all the tanks " touched down " on the beaches. The naval crews of the small craft displayed outstanding gallantry when the time came to take off the Canadian and other troops who fought ashore at Dieppe.

The success or otherwise of the Dieppe operation is not a matter for discussion here, but one thing is perfectly plain : we learnt lessons in the hard school of experience which helped materially towards the success of later and very much larger landing operations and ultimately in the storming of a way into the European mainland.

The North Africa landings led the way into the Mediterranean, and many of the ships that made the triumph of D Day possible had a record behind them from these operations and the landings on the Italian mainland, which, to be maintained, required a very high standard.

With justifiable pride, Mr. A. V. Alexander, First Lord of the Admiralty, declared after the opening of the Sicilian campaign, " In under a year the Navy have mounted and successfully carried out two of the greatest seaborne assaults in the history of warfare."

In the first forty-eight hours of the attack on Sicily, Allied naval forces had landed 80,000 men, 7,000 vehicles, 700 guns and 300 tanks of the Seventh and Eighth

Armies. In the course of the thirty-nine days' campaign on the island, naval guns supporting our troops ashore fired more than 20,000 rounds.

Our specialised landing vessels by this time included a large number of the remarkable L.S.T.'s (Landing Ship, Tanks) and L.S.I.'s (Landing Ship, Infantry). These ships, ten times the size of the landing craft, had been produced with amazing speed in American yards.

In appearance these vessels comply much more with the accepted lines of a ship than the smaller landing craft. This is largely due to the fact that they have shaped bows which are really two huge doors. The doors are not completely water-tight, although they take the force of the sea as the ship moves forward. Inside the doors there is a giant ramp which is water-tight and which comes down on a hinge in the same way as the much smaller ramps of the L.C.T.'s.

The carrying capacity of the L.S.T.'s is little short of phenomenal. They can be loaded through the deck like ordinary ships or can take on their cargoes by vehicles running directly into the ship over the ramp. Inside the ship nothing is allowed to interfere with the need for loading space. Every inch of the hold is clear of obstructions and to stand in one of these " interiors " is like being in a big hall, or, when it is artificially lighted, a cinema.

Between the side of the ship and this main space is a narrow lining in which folding bunks are arranged and rows of wash-basins are fixed for the use of the troops taking passage.

Here is the record of one landing ship, tanks, prior to D Day, which can be taken as representative of the work done by these vessels :

Sicily.—Totals carried in eight loads : 500 vehicles, 100 officers, 2,500 other ranks.

Reggio.—Totals carried in five loads : 358 vehicles, 52 officers, 1,516 other ranks.

Salerno.—Totals carried in nine loads ; 615 vehicles, 106 officers, 2,736 other ranks.

Ajaccio.—Totals carried in three loads : 200 ·vehicles, 25 officers, 696 other ranks.

Anzio.—Totals carried in two loads : 120 vehicles, 20 officers, 410 other ranks.

It will be seen that altogether this one tank landing ship transported, in the course of twenty-seven voyages, 1,793 vehicles, 303 officers and 7,858 other ranks. She served the 8th Army, the 5th Army, the Allied Air Forces and the Free French.

The capacity and usefulness of these ships were therefore fully proved before they came to their greatest task of all on D Day.

In many other directions, as the time for the main invasion drew near, the Navy sought to pave the way. In the Atlantic, where the Germans were trying desperately to inflict heavy losses on the vast supply line from the United States and Canada, the escort groups offered no quarter to the U-boats. Exactly two months before D Day the Germans themselves admitted that twenty-five more U-boats had been sunk and five were long overdue. Some of these no doubt fell to the British and Canadian air patrols, but it constituted a crippling blow at a moment when any large-scale enemy successes might have affected the time-table of our attack.

Of the part played by the Merchant Navies of the Allies it can be said that without their devoted services not only in the few months before June, 1944, but winter and summer through four years, the misnamed Second Front would not have been a practical proposition at any time.

Even with the fleets of landing ships and craft manned by naval personnel it was obvious that the Merchant Navy would have front-line work to do in the invasion. From November, 1943, onwards every M.N. man returning to Britain was given the opportunity to volunteer for invasion duties. The Combined Office of Merchant Navy Operations (it soon became known as " Comno ") put special conditions before the men, including a comprehensive system of pay.

The officers and men who volunteered—and there were very few who did not—signed a form headed " Mass Invasion of the Continent." Their Merchant Navy identity cards were marked with a " V " stamp, and they agreed to certain conditions which gave " Comno " the right to move a man from ship to ship. They signed for the duration of the Invasion operations and agreed to an entirely new system of pay which gave them a consolidated rate of overtime of thirty shillings a week for officers and twenty shillings a week for men. They became units in Britain's Merchant Navy Operational Pool.

The Merchant Navy has always guarded its liberties. These were maintained as far as possible in the Invasion organisation, but where temporary sacrifices were necessary in order that every man might be used to the best advantage, they were willingly accepted by British merchant seamen who, to their everlasting credit, sailed on D Day and subsequently as a 100 per cent. volunteer service.

The spirit that existed in our seamen, Royal Navy and Merchant Navy alike in these portentous days was equally present in the co-operating sea forces of our most powerful ally, the United States.

I was particularly impressed only a few days before we set sail for France to hear what Admiral King, Commander-in-Chief of the U.S. Navy, had written in a letter to a friend. Although it was not intended for publication, it was a call to every man and woman in America. The Admiral wrote :

" War is a tough, grim affair, and I think very likely the country as a whole can stand being toughened to the realities involved. I do not mean that we must be merely physically tough. We must be tough in our thinking, tough in our ability to make the necessary sacrifices (about which so much is said), tough at the conference table, and, in addition, tough with ourselves. In other words, I think we should be tough about everything that tends to keep us from being tough ! This country was founded, and has been maintained, by rugged people. And it is my belief that the present generation must be rugged to preserve it. It is not enough for that characteristic to be confined to the members of the Armed Forces."

In less than a month I was to see with my own eyes how tough another American admiral could be when commanding a combined Anglo-American naval force off Cherbourg, but that is a story which is told later.

Both in United States and British ports, Americans, many of them in the U.S. Army, put in an Invasion spurt which produced remarkable results.

This is what happened during the month of May, 1944, in one U.S. Army port command where both military and civilian labour was employed. The organisation moved 363,755 tons of war material, which was 170,000 tons more than was ever handled before in the ports of that area over a similar period. And the average age of the civilians was fifty-eight !

Many of the Service men had never had any experience of stevedoring before. They included peace-time lawyers, teachers, accountants, clerks, and petrol-station attendants, but, working alongside British labour, they got " right on top of the job." One Liberty ship was stowed in six days, although normally twelve or thirteen days would be required. During May, thousands of railway trucks full of war supplies were unloaded and the number of motor vehicles also ran into very high figures.

It has been set on record by the U.S. War Shipping Administration that during this time the cargoes coming from the United States included everything from munitions, tanks, guns and fighter planes to nail-polish remover for the W.A.C.'s Ships were loaded according to plan, so that priority materials would automatically come first in the unloading of each cargo. Under the schedule, each ship had a specific destination to be reached at a specific hour. When unloaded, every vehicle aboard was equipped and ready for action.

In this determination not to fail the fighting men, major difficulties were overcome, very often in the most amazing manner. One Liberty ship, laden with tanks, ran aground. To save time, U.S. Army men, who had never before worn any part of a diving suit, became amateur divers and went below the flooded decks to get the cargo out of the ship.

On another occasion there was a shortage of drivers after a number of vehicles had been landed. Sailors in the guns' crews of the Liberty ships volunteered to drive the vehicles to their destinations. The offer was accepted and the sailors made a fifty-miles journey to " deliver the goods."

When an oil purifier was needed in a hurry and it was found that it could not be obtained in Britain, a cable was sent to the United States and the required piece of mechanism arrived in England by air four days later.

So vast was the pre-invasion organisation on sea, land and in the air that it is impossible to give more than these glimpses of how inevitably the great tide rolled forward.

For the combined operation many of the best brains in the Services were devoted solely to planning and organising the Invasion for eighteen months before it took place.

It has been said that by the end of 1942, though many tactical, administrative and technical " snags " were still destined to emerge, the British General Staff had a clear picture of the basic factors which must be considered in any landings in Western Europe. In particular, the problems both of assault and maintenance (complicated by the tide factor) in offensives which might have to be sustained for a considerable period across beaches, led to the conclusion that for a combined operation on a scale unprecedented in history, against coasts which the enemy had had years to fortify, it would be necessary to provide in immense numbers special naval craft and other naval weapons and equipment, including troop-carrying aircraft.

A vital decision on the highest plane was that made at the Casablanca Conference early in 1943, when it was agreed to give first priority to clearing the Mediterranean sea route and efforts to knock Italy out of the war. It was clear then that our existing resources in specialised landing craft would be largely absorbed by these operations. At that time, too, the toll taken by enemy U-boats in sinkings of Allied shipping was still sufficiently serious to place a limit on the shipbuilding facilities which could be made available for the production of landing craft. While it was recognised that the opening of a second front in the West would have to wait until 1944, it was decided that active preparations should commence forthwith, and that a firm plan should be made as soon as possible.

In March, 1943, the Chief of Staff to a future Supreme Allied Commander was appointed, and he was provided with an Anglo-American planning staff of all the three services. The plan evolved was approved by Mr. Churchill and President Roosevelt at the Quebec Conference. in August, 1943.

In January, 1944, General Eisenhower became Supreme Commander. Under him, Admiral Ramsay controlled the final build-up of the amazingly intricate naval organisation, and as the days lengthened towards mid-summer we found ourselves at last on the eve of great and historic events across the Channel.

THE KING SAW THESE ASSAULT LANDING CRAFT IN MASSED FORMATION SHORTLY BEFORE D DAY

THE LANDING ON THE NORMAN
From the painting by C. E. Turner, by permiss

...AST, LOOKING WESTWARD
"*The Illustrated London News*"

OFF THE SOUTHERN COAST OF ENGLAND AS D DAY APPROACHED

(Royal Canadian Navy Photograph)

II

THE WAITING ARMADA

They mark our passage as a race of men,
Earth will not see such ships as those again.
JOHN MASEFIELD.

II

THE WAITING ARMADA

DURING the last two or three months before the Invasion actually took place there was one thing I was quite certain about—tension was at a much higher pitch among the general public than in the armed forces.

In naval circles there was a sense of expectancy and a quiet confidence.

It reminded me of the young subaltern of the Manchester Regiment who was at Wavre, in Belgium, when the first shells from German artillery whistled over the British army in this war. Having moved into Belgium at the very last moment, the men of the Manchesters were still sandbagging windows and digging machine-gun posts when the full weight of the German army descended upon them. They could not even make use of the pill-boxes built by the Belgians because the entrances had been made too narrow to admit a British anti-tank gun. The Manchesters were in anything but a happy situation, but when I spoke with some sympathy, the young officer brushed it aside with, " Why, this is just what we came here for—to fight ! "

So, in 1944, there was no need for tension among the fighting men because they were merely going to have the opportunity to do what they all wanted to do—play a part in the final cleaning up of the Huns.

Young men who were still at school when the war started, accepted what was immediately ahead of them as a natural responsibility. To one who had observed at first hand all through the war, a big change in attitude from that of earlier days was apparent. There was not much glory left in war for these young men. They had seen its horrors in cities and towns even before they began to train as fighters.

Perhaps it was this background of memory, stronger

than any of the far-off and almost childish recollections
of peace-time, that enabled them to handle their arms
with a cold-blooded and scientific efficiency. Long ago
the shouting had died away and war had become for
them a business in which they were determined to succeed.
If for no other reason, failure was out of the question
because of the comrades, known and unknown, who had
handed on the torch. While they smiled at the last-war
phrase, " War to end wars," they thought of the generation that would follow them, and willingly risked and
gave their lives in the unspoken hope that a better world
might be built up in the years to come by those who
were left to carry on.

By the time May came it was obvious to everyone in
the services, even remotely concerned with the forthcoming attack, that " it was any day now."

The sea, as was inevitable, had provided many problems
apart from the major one of transportation. For instance,
it was essential that thousands of vehicles should be able
to take a wetting and yet be in condition to go straight
into battle. The Navy assisted the Army Directorate of
Mechanical Engineering to find a solution to the problem
of " waterproofing." A car or lorry can pass safely
through a shallow stream, but when it comes to amphibious operations conducted from the sea, provision must
be made not only for deep and possibly rough water,
but also for the corrosive effects of salt. The exhausts
of some of the tanks were therefore extended and raised
like funnels until they were as high as the turrets.

Waterproofing had also to be extended to the vulnerable
contents of an immense list of special military vehicles,
ranging from office trucks to self-propelled artillery.
Recovery units had to be prepared to work in considerable
depths of water.

In the final stages of preparation there was a most
important link-up between the disposition of ships and
landing-craft and the drafting of army units into the
special marshalling areas near the coast. When an army
is dispatched overseas for operations in a distant sphere,

large transports are employed, on some of which a complete Brigade can be accommodated. The final tactical dispositions in such a case can be done, and usually are done, in the ship.

For shore-to-shore attacks over comparatively limited stretches of water, however, dispositions must be made before the troops are embarked in the landing craft. The first wave of the assault must land, as far as possible, in the form of self-supporting combat teams. In the case of the forces that follow, it is desirable that risks from enemy action during the passage should be spread by distributing among the assault craft, infantry, gunners, sappers and the numerous other branches of the modern army.

The marshalling-area mechanism—known to Movements staffs as " the mincing machine "—must break up units and provide mixed loads for the various forms of sea transport.

The marshalling areas themselves are dependent, as to size, on the capacity of the embarkation areas they are to serve. Units passing on from the marshalling camps lose their identity and become serially numbered components of craft or ship loads.

For D Day, and subsequently, Movement Control was responsible for this arrangement. In two sub-divisions (" Sector " and " Embarkation ") it was also responsible for traffic at the " hards " and for embarkation of the Force and its assault vehicles into craft. A Unit Sheet showed the battalion, battery or squadron commander exactly how to split his unit into parties for embarkation in different craft. A Ship Sheet showed the craft load commander (not to be confused with the naval commander of the vessel) exactly what unit parties went to make up his command.

The whole movement was co-ordinated not merely from marshalling area to craft, but seawards right from the concentration area, by an Inter-Service organisation known as " Build-up Control." There were three parts of this Control, one of which was " Turn-round Control "

—a naval staff organisation which was responsible for the execution of " Built-up Control's " plans in terms of assault craft and shipping movement. It was necessary that the whole of this elaborate set-up should function smoothly twenty-four hours a day and seven days a week.

It was possible to pre-load craft without too great a rush for the first flight of the assault. Long in advance, loading tables had been prepared by Brigade and unit staffs. These showed detailed tactical loading requirements to fit the needs of the plan of attack.

For the " follow-up " and " build-up " forces, a much more flexible mechanism had to come into operation. They had to meet requirements according to the development of the battle.

And all this merely describes the main trunk of the embarkation tree. For each of the services there were many small but important off-shoots.

Public Relations might be regarded as one of them, and the thoroughness with which preparations for the covering of the Invasion and subsequent events were made provides an interesting sidelight on the whole organisation.

Firstly, it became known that " Shaef " (the shortened name for Supreme Headquarters, Allied Expeditionary Force) would give special accreditation to correspondents, quite apart from whether they already had similar recognition from Navy, Army or Air Force. Brigadier Turner, of the British Army, and a U.S. army officer of similar rank, were to command the Shaef P.R. unit, which was also to have its own censorship, under the direction of Colonel Warden; whose experience went back to the days of the B.E.F. in France.

Coming at a late stage in the war, it was a rather startling development, especially for the British correspondents who, for four and a half years, had functioned under Admiralty, War Office or Air Ministry control.

Some, including myself, felt a pride in the Licences which we had carried all through the war. In my case the little blue book had been issued to me on the 10th of October, 1939, and bore the number " 19." It also had the signature of the first Adjutant-General of a British Army in the field in this war, and in other ways held a sentimental value. We were not anxious to surrender these tattered records for an entirely new set of credentials.

These were incidental things, however, and eventually we attended an accreditation ceremony in a big room in London which was being prepared to take maps all round the wall. As we waited to give particulars to American Army clerks we tried to guess what countries and what coast areas would be depicted on the large-scale maps when they eventually appeared on the walls.

Most of the questions asked by Shaef had been answered a hundred times before during the war by correspondents, but there was one new query : " To what blood group do you belong ? " It was a very practical question in view of the risks of the forthcoming campaign and the proved value of blood transfusions to wounded men.

As I was taking a few days leave immediately after the visit to Press Headquarters, I promised to provide them with the answer. I would have been more ready to wait for the Service procedure in this matter if I had known how much time had to be spent as a civilian to get the answer to what should be a commonplace question these days.

I was in a Surrey village, not thirty miles from London. Having discovered the times at which a doctor visited the village, I went to see him. There was nothing that he could do about it personally. He proposed that I should go to a hospital. The village is two miles from the nearest station, but it is linked to a market town by a regular bus service. The market town, however, is in Sussex, so the doctor, to avoid inter-county complications, although I wished to pay whatever fee was charged, said it would be better if I went to the hospital in the nearest Surrey town, seven miles away.

When I arrived there they very politely told me that they had no serum and it would be necessary to continue my journey for several more miles to another town—if an appointment could be made for that day. It was made, and, after arriving at the wrong hospital in the next town, I sat in a chair, felt a pin-prick in the lobe of my ear, saw the minute sample of blood tested, and in five minutes had exchanged seven and sixpence for a slip of paper on which the answer to the blood-group question was written.

One learned long ago that complaining in war-time helps nobody but the enemy—but two of my precious days had gone in this search !

The next summons to correspondents was exciting. We were to meet Admiral Ramsay, supreme commander of Allied naval forces under General Eisenhower.

About fifty correspondents, mostly British, American or Canadian, assembled to hear the Admiral's " off-the-record " talk. The U.S. correspondents were in khaki, and this, it was subsequently suggested, accounted for all naval correspondents, with, as far as I know, one exception, wearing khaki on D Day.

As the Admiralty had never been able to evolve a proper uniform for the men who go to sea to report and, of necessity, take exactly the same risk as those who fight, one suspected that they were only too glad to accept the excuse offered by the khaki-clad Americans. As a considerable concession on the part of the powers-that-be, they presented each naval correspondent with one pair of green tabs, three inches long by three-quarters of an inch wide, bearing the word " Naval " which were to be worn on the shoulder. As most correspondents had at least two uniforms, they went about with one shoulder of each decorated and had to pivot smartly on the heel to show off the one tiny label which indicated that they had an association with a Service which was to cost at least one of them his life in the course of a few days.

The conference with Admiral Ramsay was a real

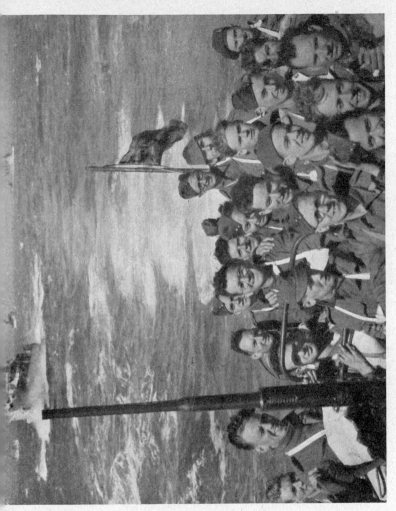

"WHITE HORSES" FAIL TO UPSET BRITISH INFANTRY ON THE WAY IN

(Royal Canadian Navy Photograph)

PART OF THE INVASION FLEET SETS OUT

(Royal Canadian Navy Photograph)

success, although, I understand, the Admiral went away from it with the belief that he was leaving behind a large party of disappointed correspondents. This situation arose because the Admiral, sharp-eyed and almost nervously quick of speech, spoke so fully and frankly of all angles of Press and Radio " coverage " of the naval side of the Second Front, and the facilities that were being provided for us, that not a single question was forthcoming at the end of the conference, although we were discussing the most momentous naval operation of the war.

Later we received credentials, in the form of two letters, which were the most comprehensive ever given to correspondents during the war.

General Eisenhower, the Supreme Commander, wrote : " To all Unit Commanders, Allied Expeditionary Force. At my first Press Conference as Supreme Commander I told the War Correspondents that once they were accredited to my headquarters I considered then quasi-staff officers. All war correspondents that may accompany the expedition are first accredited to Supreme Headquarters and operate under policies approved by the Supreme Command. They are, in turn, assigned to lower headquarters in accordance with agreements between the Public Relations Division of this head-quarters and the Public Relations officers on the staffs of the several Commanders-in-Chief. This allocation is always limited by accommodation available. Public Relations officers of the various echelons act as their guides. As a matter of policy, accredited war correspondents should be accorded the greatest possible latitude in the gathering of legitimate news. Consequently it is desired that, subject always to the requirements of operations, of which the Commander on the spot must be the sole judge, Commanders of all echelons and Public Relations officers and Conducting officers give accredited war correspondents all reasonable assistance. They should be allowed to talk freely with officers and enlisted personnel and to see the machinery of war in operation in order to visualise and transmit to the public the conditions under which the men from their countries are waging war against the enemy."

In a covering letter, Admiral Ramsay stated : " The attention of Commanding Officers of all ships and craft to which War Correspondents are accredited, is drawn to the attached letter from the Supreme Commander, General Eisenhower. It is the duty of all Commanding Officers to see that accredited war correspondents, on production of their licence, are given every help, and further to assist them in dispatching their copy, both written and photographic material, to the United Kingdom by the quickest possible means consistent with operational needs."

The value of such documents can well be appreciated, and as the Press directly represents the great public, which cannot receive the facilities itself, it is a matter of both interest and importance to the average citizen that the Press should be so fully provided for.

In order to preserve the continuity of events, I will continue to tell the story of the correspondents up to the point of their embarkation on June 2nd.

There was one " false alarm," when all the naval correspondents were assembled, conveyed to home ports, and put aboard various ships and craft. After a few hours, the party returned to London.

On the morning of Friday, June 2nd, when, in accordance with instructions received only a few hours earlier, we reported to the Admiralty, there was no doubt that we were being mobilised for the " real thing."

Driving through London on that bright, sunny morning, I looked at the old familiar landmarks with a re-awakened interest. Marks of war there were everywhere—soon to be added to by the uncontrolled flying bombs—but much remained the same after years of trial. Crossing Putney Bridge, I noted the famous boathouses away on the left as the river sweeps round to Hammersmith. In one of them, surrounded by the records and trophies of generations of " Thames " men, I had met only a few weeks before, scores of South-West London youngsters wearing the smart uniforms of the Sea Cadets. They were all training with heart and soul so that they might have a measure of efficiency when they entered the Royal Navy.

The big building of the London Rowing Club, so often used by Oxford during their final preparations for the University Boat Race, had, I knew, a not unusual war-time sign displayed on its broad balcony—FIRE STATION.

On the Fulham side of the bridge stood the fine parish church, nestled in the green background of the trees in Bishop's Park. I wondered for the hundredth time about the truth of the story that this church and the smaller one on the Putney side of the bridge were built in rivalry by two sisters.

What I did know was that behind the long fringe of riverside trees stood old Fulham Palace, home of Bishops of London through the centuries. I pictured the red-brick courtyard with its atmosphere of carriages and phætons. The moat that surrounded the Palace, I remembered, had been filled in years ago. It was said to have become somewhat odorous, but I, as a boy, found it altogether fascinating and was very much on the side of those who sought to preserve it—smell and all.

The little houses of Fulham, largely a London dormitory borough, clean and tidy despite the bomb scars spread among them, brought one back to the present. From each one of these regimented streets men had gone out to fight ; many of them, no doubt, would come back to tell of D Day—and some would not return.

It was from these streets, as from the rest of mighty London, and every city, town and hamlet of the land, that men had gone to swell the chorus :

> " Use me, England,
> in thine hour of need,
> Let thy ruling
> rule me now in deed."

and if necessary they would go further and say :

> " Give then, England,
> if my life thou need,
> Gift yet fairer,
> Death, thy life to feed."

These were in no way sad thoughts as one passed through London on that pleasant June morning. Had not the very women and children that walked in the streets faced death almost equally with the fighting men. Never before had so many joined in a common cause against oppression and tyranny. And now all would play their part in the great climax so close at hand.

*   *   *   *   *   *

In a big conference-room at the Admiralty I found even more correspondents than had listened to Admiral Ramsay. Among them, to mention but a few, were Captain Russell Grenfell, Commander Peter McRichie and Lieut.-Commander George Lawrence (of the Royal Canadian Navy Press department), Arthur Thorpe, A. J. McWhinnie, Michael Standing and Richard North (of the B.B.C.), John Marshall, " Jimmy " Southcott, Desmond Tighe and W. A. Crumley.

The Canadians, as serving officers, wore naval uniform. All the others were in khaki, with the exception of Captain Russell Grenfell, who admitted frankly that he could not bring himself to wear anything but blue for such an auspicious occasion. He therefore wore naval uniform without any markings of rank.

On the big table in the centre of the room were a number of sealed letters. One was addressed to each correspondent. Inside, written on a printed Admiralty permit, was the information we all wanted—the name of the ship in which we were to take passage.

I opened mine and read H.M.S. *Hilary*. For a moment I was nonplussed. I did not recognise the name and I had expected to be able to place at once the class of ship in which I was to sail. The answer was supplied by

Desmond Tighe. It was a converted merchant ship which was now used as a headquarters ship. I counted myself lucky and compared notes with other correspondents who were to sail in destroyers, landing craft, M.T.B.'s and every type of vessel.

Commander John Dillon Robinson, Shaef Staff Press Liaison officer, then gave the first operational " briefing."

We learned that the forces engaged in the operation would consist of two task forces—to be known as the Western and Eastern Task Forces. The Western force would be commanded by Rear-Admiral Alan G. Kirk, of the U.S. Navy, and the Eastern Force by Rear-Admiral Sir Philip Vian, of the Royal Navy. Each force would consist of an assault force, a follow-up force, a bombarding force and minesweeping flotillas. Each task force would be a complete unit in itself and the two commanders would come under the overall command of the Allied Naval Commander-in-Chief.

The object in both cases was simple : it was the landing of military forces in their respective sectors.

The Western task force was to be composed, in the main of United States ships and the Eastern force of British vessels. Most Canadian ships would be in the eastern force, although a R.C.N. minesweeping flotilla would be with the Americans.

The bombarding forces would be a mixture.

In the Eastern task force there were to be three naval assault forces and one follow-up force. On the other flank there were to be two naval assault forces and a follow-up force.

The warships and larger vessels involved, down to the L.S.I.'s, would be 75 per cent. British, but the over-all percentage, which included all the smaller craft, was given as 60 per cent. British and 40 per cent. American.

We were left a little breathless by other figures which were divulged to us. The total number of ships and craft engaged would be over four thousand, not including the hundreds of small craft carried to the enemy occupied coast in other vessels. Over eighty ships would take part in the bombardment and more than six hundred guns, from 4-inch to 16-inch, would open fire. It was calculated that at the actual time of the assault over two thousand tons of high explosives would go down on the enemy in ten minutes from the naval guns alone.

Admiral Ramsay, we were told, had expressed a particular wish that a full account should be given of the work of the British and United States Merchant navies. But for the work which they would do afterwards the efforts of the fighting ships would be useless.

Then we heard the names of some of the famous ships taking part. A more complete list can be given later, but names such as the *Warspite, Nelson, Rodney, Ramilles, Glasgow, Enterprise, Orion* and *Onslow* in the British list, *Arkansas, Texas, Nevada, Tuscaloosa, Augusta* and *Quincy* in the U.S.N. list and *Sioux* and *Algonquin* among the Canadian ships, left no doubt that the Allied Navies were out to hit a terrific blow.

The names of the naval force commanders were given, including Rear-Admiral A. G. Talbot, D.S.O., R.N., Rear-Admiral W. E. Parry, C.B., R.N., Rear-Admiral Moon, U.S.N., Commodore Douglas-Pennant, C.B.E., R N., Commodore G. N. Oliver, D.S.O., R.N., and Commodore Edgar, U.S.N.

Even at this late stage it was necessary to give a quick review of the types of ships and craft that would be engaged in the assault. To get all the odd letters to which their names had been abbreviated at one's fingertips was like learning a jumbled form of twice-times tables. It ran more or less along these lines :

L.C.A.'s are Landing Craft, Assault, often launched from

L.S.I.'s, Landing Ship, Infantry.

L.C.I.'s are Landing Craft, Infantry, and are

(L.) large or (S.) small. They have ramps in front and the troops wade ashore from them.

L.C.T.'s are Landing Craft, Tanks, and carry tanks or vehicles. They are snub-nosed with a ramp which goes down for the vehicles to pass over.

L.S.T.'s are Landing Ships, Tanks, and are large vessels capable of carrying 80 vehicles and 360 men. Their bows open like doors, a ramp goes down and the tanks roll out.

Rhino ferry craft are made to all sizes by the joining up of any number of hollow metal sections. Can be used as huge floating rafts or, inshore, as landing stages.

L.C.T.R.'s are landing craft specially equipped for firing Rockets.

L.C.G.'s are specially equipped with Guns.

L.C.F.'s are Landing Craft, Flak.

L.C.T.C.B.'s are Landing Craft, Tanks, Concrete Busters.

L.C.S.'s are Landing Craft, Support.

L.C.K.'s are Landing Craft, Kitchens.

L.S.H.'s are Landing Ship, Headquarters.

" Ducks " are amphibious craft capable of being used as boats or lorries.

And the table is still far from complete.

The briefing of the correspondents concluded with the quoting of words used a few days earlier by the Chief of Staff to Admiral Ramsay, at a momentous conference : " Gentlemen, what Philip of Spain failed to do, what Napoleon tried and failed to do and what Hitler never had the courage to try, we are about to do, and with God's grace we shall."

Then began what might be termed the first real invasion journey for the men who were to tell the whole world about a day that will live as long as history books are read.

No doubt we were somewhat excited, but nobody could say that the journey was exciting. In two very uncomfortable wooden-seated coaches we drove all the way to Portsmouth and Southampton. As McWhinnie said, there would be no need for identification discs for the correspondents. After sitting on those seats for several hours four broad stripes on a certain part of our anatomy would remain as a lasting identity mark !

Riding with me was Lieut.-Commander George Lawrence, recently arrived from Canada in order to be an official observer of the invasion. He capped McWhinnie's crack by saying that it was the only way four stripes were ever likely to come to him.

Twice on our journey to the coast we stopped to obtain refreshment. The first occasion was at the " Master Robert," on the Great West Road. The good lady of the house did her war-time best for us, and although nobody was talking of the things we had just heard, she may have sensed that this was no ordinary occasion. She came to see us off, and I think there were tears in her eyes as she waved and repeated, " Good luck, boys, good luck ! "

Much farther on our journey we stopped again and went into a hotel with a delightful lounge full of deep, chintz-covered arm-chairs. From the haughty surprise with which we were greeted by three middle-aged ladies we might have been German officers arriving in their retreat. Unless we sat down to a five-shilling meal which we did not want, the hotel had no refreshment to offer us, so we did not disturb them for long.

Long before we arrived in Southampton we were in the thick of one of the amazing invasion assembly areas. We drove between and among ever-thickening lines of tanks, guns, vehicles and troops. The men looked brown and fit and, in some curious way, relaxed, like an athlete in the last few hours before a contest for which he has trained for weeks.

Southampton itself was chock-a-block with fighting material, but not once did I see a bad hold-up. Moving columns went through steadily to the loading points, while others lined the roads and waited for their turn to join the stream.

Our take-off point was from near the Pier, so well-known to Isle of Wight holiday-makers in peace-time. As we approached it we saw the first of the big tank and infantry landing ships nosed into specially constructed " hards " (concrete loading slopes). The doors in their bows were open, and through these gaping mouths they swallowed tanks and men in prodigious quantities.

Our party split up into various boats which were awaiting us. There were hand-shakes and quips about how we would celebrate when we returned, and then the boats headed down Southampton Water towards the Solent.

The *Hilary* was anchored not far from the Isle of Wight, and the long run to her provided one with an unforgettable panorama of ships and craft, the great majority of which had a single purpose—invasion. A landing craft anchorage off the mainland continued until it was out of sight. These hundreds, probably thousands, of flat-bottomed craft, all alike and with a network of low-flying silver balloons over them, made the most extraordinary assembly of vessels I have ever seen.

A comparison flashed through my mind with the rag-tag and bobtail collection of craft which straggled across the sea to and from Dunkirk. Four years is a long time, but looking at that staggering assembly of modern invasion vessels, it seemed a short period in which to bring about such enormous changes in the situation at sea.

Some of the L.C.T.'s out in the stream were already loaded with tanks, the soldiers sunning themselves on top of the turrets. Loaded L.S.T.'s were there also, their decks crowded with vehicles in addition to the dozens carried in their interiors. One, flying the Stars and Stripes, carried many motor ambulances. Another had an entire cargo of portable bridge sections.

Most of the ships had the British patchwork system of camouflage, but there were vessels with the neater twin shading in grey-blues which has been largely used by the Americans. Both the Solent and Spithead were crammed with shipping, although sufficient space had been left between the ships to give them a good chance of escaping damage should the Germans attempt any last-minute desperation attacks by air.

The party for H.M.S. *Hilary* consisted of David McNichol, an Australian correspondent who had returned, to reporting the war after two years of fighting it in the Western Desert; Bert Clark, an American representing the Blue Broadcasting Network; Michael Standing, of the B.B.C., his mechanic, Jack Fonville, and myself.

The *Hilary*, we found, bore very little resemblance to a warship. There had been a good deal of conversion internally to fit her for her rôle as a headquarters ship, but her merchant ship lines had hardly been changed at all. She was one of the few coal-burning ships of the invasion fleet, but she was still very spic and span, and there was no mistaking the atmosphere of the Navy from her commanding officer, Captain Sir James Paget, Bart., R.N., to the latest joined "H.O."

She was the headquarters ship of Commodore G. N. Oliver and, more temporarily, of a Canadian Army Assault force and an R.A.F. command presided over by a group captain.

Their staffs, added to the ships officers, meant that cabin space in the *Hilary* was at a premium. We were in no way dissatisfied when we were given a curtained-off part of the big ward-room as our sleeping space. We arranged our camp beds on a platform, normally used for ward-room concerts, and got a good laugh when Michael Standing, who is 6 feet 5 inches in height, tried out his bed and found (1) that he overlapped by a foot or more, and (2) that he had settled down on the ship's cat, which had taken refuge from the general bustle going on in the ship under the low camp bed.

During the evening we met the Chief Steward, a Merchant Navy sailor of long standing and a notable character in the ship, who was delighted to discuss Australia with McNichol, and even more delighted to produce odd bits of Australian scandal which made the correspondent exclaim, "Now, how did you know that?"

Then we went to bed and slept well in our curtained-off dormitory.

III

OFF TO NORMANDY!

Our life is closed, our life begins,
The long, long anchorage we leave,
The ship is clear at last, she leaps!
She swiftly courses from the shore,
Joy, shipmate, joy.

WALT WHITMAN

CHAPTER III

OFF TO NORMANDY!

SOLDIERS always look a little out of place in a ship, with the exception of the Navy's own soldiers—the Royal Marines.

A soldier taken to sea is very much an innocent abroad, and, in my experience, is always ready to admit it. He is conscious of the lack of space and of his own awkwardness in comparison with the sailor. In his heavy boots he clod-hops up and down gangways which the sailor negotiates with the light-footedness of a dancing master. He has not got the knack of balancing himself at all times to meet the movement of the ship, and as a result often makes his journeys around the deck in short, involuntary runs between one fixed object and another. If he is laden with the weight of heavy equipment high up on his shoulders, sooner or later he is almost bound to upset.

And as the sea is a great leveller, officers suffer the same inconveniences as their men.

Practically all the Canadian soldiers in H.M.S. *Hilary* were officers, it being a headquarters ship. Nearly all of them were fine, big men physically, which may have added to their difficulties because there were some who moved around the ship like good-humoured young bulls. They were in magnificent spirits, knowing that the moment they had awaited so long was at hand, and metaphorically rolling up their sleeves in anticipation.

They could even joke about the prospect. Said one young Canadian, sitting with a bunch of brother officers, " What about us writing to my wife ? Let's give her the low-down on all our weapons—maybe that will get us out of this thing ! "—a sally which was greeted with a roar of laughter.

45

Attached to the Canadian headquarters party was my friend Ross Monro, whose graphic accounts of front-line Canadian fighters are so well known in the Dominion. Tall and bespectacled, Munro has lived the life of a soldier from the time he came to this country early in the war and stood by to go with the Canadian troops who would have been one of the main defences of Britain if the Germans had attacked this island.

He was ashore at Dieppe with his countrymen and was now ready again to storm up the beaches very close to the first wave of assault troops. In his earnest, straightforward way he told me that the Canadians counted it an honour to have been entrusted with the initial assault. " They won't let you down," he said, treating me as the representative of our own crack assault troops, many of whom had had the battle experience which the Canadians lacked. And I replied, " You need not say it, Ross, I know they will not."

In my mind's eye I saw the split column of the memorial to 49,000 Canadians which dominates the bloody ridge at Vimy. The sons of those men would not permit their sacrifice to have been made in vain.

That evening, Saturday, June 3rd, which, according to the original plans, would have been the last evening in home waters for thousands of men, if D Day had not been put back twenty-four hours, gave me one of the most thrilling experiences of my life.

We were taken ashore as an escorted party, the ship being " sealed," and the colonel commanding the Canadian assault forces—I believe he was well under forty—unfolded the whole picture of events which, in the next forty-eight hours, would stir the world. For nearly three hours I was held spellbound while the curtain was lifted, and I looked at the plan of future happenings that would vitally affect hundreds of thousands of human beings.

It is not the purpose of this book to deal with the military development of the invasion, but, in setting on record the briefing given to a handful of correspondents by the Canadian Colonel, I can indicate both the D-Day objectives of the combined forces on one important sector of the beaches and, from the army side, show the dependence of the military forces on our sea supremacy.

Sitting in a half-circle in a bare room, with the young Colonel talking to us quietly across the table, this, in effect, is what we heard :

Planning for the invasion has been going on for a considerable time, and for the last six months we have done nothing else. It simply could not be put on one day earlier than it is being put on. There was no tide to contend with in the Mediterranean operations. Here the tides have been a terrific problem, especially for the Navy. The Germans, we believe, expect any invasion attempt we make to take place at high tide. It will happen about four hours before high water. The movement control organisation has had to be set up from scratch, but the biggest problem of all has been security. After General Montgomery had considered the military plans, following his return from his other campaigns, some radical changes had to be made.

The technique of the Canadians was developed in exercises based mostly on the lessons learned at Dieppe (we heard). Each Division is practically a Corps ; it is not an Infantry Division but an Armoured Division with self-propelled guns. " Swimming " tanks will be the first to go in, followed by Churchill tanks with all sorts of special gadgets on them. In some of the early craft there will be armoured bulldozers, which will help to deal with the innumerable mined obstacles. At H plus 5 the first infantry go in. The fire-support programme will have started at H minus 40 minutes. About H minus 20 to H minus 10 the bombers, five squadrons of Fortresses, will have dropped their loads where each infantry assault is being made. Three hundred and sixty tons of bombs will be dropped on our immediate objects. Self-propelled artillery, firing as they go in, will put down about another 150 tons. They will be followed by the rocket ships. All fire support stops at H hour.

Right smack in the middle of our beaches is the mouth of a river (the story continued). There is a town there, too. We hope to have our first objectives by H plus One, although it will be H plus Three and a half to Four before the artillery are ashore. By the time they are there we hope the infantry will be up to the intermediate objectives. The final objectives are about twelve miles inland. Tanks and bicycles will help to make the troops mobile.

Then we heard what was to be expected on the beaches and the plans made for overcoming the Nazis' first line defences : There are angle-irons and hedgehogs, everyone of them with a mine on top, and a line of wooden posts with mines or shells on some of them. In front of that there is a sort of cement obstacle, which is known as "element C." It is proposed to tear four gaps across the beaches, one of 600 yards, two of 400 yards, and another of 200 yards. The sappers will go in to make the first attempt to clear the obstructions. The enemy defences ashore are good. In some cases he has concealed batteries behind twelve feet of thick concrete. Machine guns sweep the beaches and there are pillboxes and concrete emplacements. The Canadians will attack on a front of 10,000 yards, and we should have overwhelming forces, with sea and air power added, to deal with the enemy on the beaches.

The final dramatic moment was when the Colonel, receiving assurances from officers present that we should not be allowed to leave the ships we were in until after the events of D Day, pulled the curtains and got out a large map. He unrolled it on the table and, for the first time, we saw the exact location of the invasion beaches.

Names, which in a few days time were to obtain a world-wide significance, stood out boldly on the large-scale map—Courseulles, St. Aubin, Arromanches, Bernieres, Port en Besin, St. Laurent. . . .

Another map showed us the full expanse of the Bay of the Seine, and we saw how the various attacks were being co-ordinated.

TEN MINUTES OFF THE BEACHES IN A CANADIAN INFANTRY LANDING SHIP
(Royal Canadian Navy Photograph)

LANDING CRAFT MAKE THE BEACHES — OR ALMOST!

(Royal Canadian Navy Photograph)

At first glance it looked as if the Allied left flank would be dangerously exposed. Then we heard of the vital part to be played by the Airborne troops to the east of the Caen Canal. The Germans were known to have big guns in the region of Le Havre, but the bombers and, if necessary, the warships would look after those.

We studied the German defences along the beaches and the strip of coast by the sea. Many of the obstructions in the sea, it appeared, were fitted with old French shells, fused to go off like mines if they were touched.

Information as to the exact nature of the German defences, particularly the beach obstructions, undoubtedly saved many lives when the moment of assault came. The information was collected in various ways. One aerial reconnaissance photograph I saw was taken from a plane skimming so low along the German-held beaches that it was possible to see the upturned faces of soldiers dashing for their lives towards points of cover. Several were attempting to hide behind the posts stuck in the sand.

What is not generally known is that daring patrols of a few picked soldiers landed on the French invasion beaches by night and obtained first-hand information of the obstructions shortly before D Day. One such patrol spent more than two hours on what, as far as the enemy was concerned, was a front-line beach, and left again without having been detected by the German look-outs.

We spent a long time looking at the Colonel's maps, and then returned to our ships. That night I was thankful for the isolating sea around me, because the secret that I now shared with a limited number of other people involved the lives of many thousands of men. I thought of the Prime Minister and others in responsible places who had carried, in addition to their responsibility, this burden of knowledge for many months.

A comment by one of the Canadian officers stuck in my mind : " We have waited so long for this thing," he said, " and had so many exercises that it is almost impossible to believe that, this time, we shall not be going back to our old billets in England. Sometimes we got very tired of waiting—that was not what we came all the way from Canada for—but now that we are off, and may not see England again before we eventually return to Canada, one remembers many happy experiences."

He mentioned particularly one jolly Christmas spent in Cheltenham. I was glad that this dignified English spa should have earned a place in the memory of those who came to fight from one of the most virile and go-ahead countries in the world to-day.

In Canada a few months earlier I had formed the opinion that, while maintaining a strong attachment for "the old country," the Dominion would go forward with sturdy independence after the war and that a magnificent future stretched ahead of her. While it is not possible to generalise about such things as climatic conditions in a country which stretches for thousands of miles, it is true that much of the Dominion has to face bitter cold during some months of the year. The fine natural harbour at Sydney, Nova Scotia, for instance, is invariably iced up, although it is south of Newfoundland. These hard weather conditions, taking the main belt of Canada and not including the northern territories, are instrumental, I believe, in producing a hardy, self-reliant race, which, given the necessary leadership, is going to make itself more and more felt in the post-war development of the world.

Many of our young men have had the opportunity, while serving their country, to see some parts of Canada for themselves. Its spaciousness and freshness has fascinated them and challenged the old pioneer spirit of the British. Numbers of them have told me that they want to go to the Dominion after the war and live there. Most of the influential Canadians I met—and I talked with members of the Government and heads of local administrations—knew that this desire existed and everywhere it found favour. Canada, they said, wanted those who, having proved themselves men under war conditions, would show the same initiative and courage in working for themselves and the community in peacetime.

But this is all a jump ahead of the work that still had to be done by the Canadians who were my shipmates.

During the morning of Sunday, June 4th, the weather steadily deteriorated. This was most disturbing, because we knew that we were on the very eve of D Day and that fine weather was one of the essential ingredients for success, or, at least, that those responsible for the final planning had counted on good weather conditions for the execution of those plans. I have been told that in one of the opening paragraphs of the orders covering the operation there was a sentence : " These operations will take place in fine weather."

Just when we wanted the almost unbroken spell of lovely weather which had marked the whole of May to continue for at least a few more days, the break came. The wind, blowing from the west, got up considerably as the morning passed. White caps appeared on the waters of the Solent and the naval men shook their heads as they looked at the scudding clouds. " It is not like crossing the Straits of Dover," they said. " It is a long journey for the landing craft. Some of them would get swamped in the conditions outside."

McNichol and I paid a visit to the Operations room in the *Hilary* and saw the big illuminated map-table on which all the movements in our sector would be recorded. Army, Navy and Air Force mixed there as one service. It was the floating nerve centre of the whole of the force, but we knew that a shadow Operations room with a shadow combined staff was not far away and would take over at once if anything happened to put the *Hilary's* " Opts " room out of action.

Odd things occupied the attention of the large number of people in the ship during these rather tense hours. A shortage of water, not uncommon in ships which have been converted and which are called upon to take large numbers of personnel, was the concern of all. For about five minutes three or four times a day the water was turned on, and then word went round like wildfire. Practically everybody made a dash for a tap, and if they had not time to use the water on the spot they carried it away in odd tins or anything that would contain it.

Hot sea water was available in the bathrooms, but only those who have tried to use it for washing purposes will know the ineffectiveness of ordinary soap and the general stickiness that results. A notable " find " by McNichol—a piece of salt-water soap—helped considerably.

The weather did not improve in the afternoon but a long line of landing craft twisted its way through the shipping off Spithead and made for the open sea. " They have got to get on their way," I was told, " because if to-morrow morning is the great day they must be some distance across the Channel before the faster ships set out."

It was the general opinion, however, that the small vessels would be recalled after an hour or two if the weather did not improve considerably. And that, no doubt, is what did happen because there was no movement for us that night.

Big flights of aircraft had passed over the anchorage during the day, heading out across the Channel. They were looked upon by the optimists as a hopeful sign. Others looked at them with envy because of the ease with which they could get to the target area.

The radio kept us informed of events in another sphere. Allied troops were approaching Rome. Highway 6 was still the scene of German resistance but the enemy were being swept aside. " By nightfall we shall know if the Germans intend to fight in Rome," said the announcer. We hoped that the troops who had fought so hard for their triumph would get to Rome in time to thrill the world with the news of their victory before D Day came to overshadow their achievement.

In the early evening Michael Standing invited me to join the *Hilary's* usual Sunday night Brains Trust with him. On the assumption that the standard of brains required would not be too high, I agreed.

Once before I had joined in a similar party, in H.M.S. *Woolston*, while she was escorting a convoy through E-boat alley on the northward run. That, I remembered, had been good fun, with a number of questions asking for the lightest possible treatment and permitting a series of personal " cracks " which delighted the crew, listening at their various action stations.

In this belief—I was soon to be disillusioned—I went to a radio room in the *Hilary* with Standing, who was to act as Question Master. It was interesting to see that the man who has broadcast to millions in such a well-known series as " Standing at the Corner of the Street," not only took his duties seriously but was almost nervous about broadcasting to the very limited, but undoubtedly critical, audience provided by the personnel of H.M.S. *Hilary*. His voice and manner gave such an authentic touch to the proceedings that more than one inquiry was made in the ship afterwards, I was told, as to whether it was a ship's broadcast or the B.B.C.

I became a little alarmed at the serious air of the whole proceedings and suggested, before the session began, that I might be regarded as a very minor Commander Campbell in the team—ready with an entertaining answer but not attempting the depths of a Huxley or Joad.

It was just as well that I made the point because when the questions were divulged one by one, they entered serious and controversial fields and would no doubt have suited the palates of the Number One Brains Trusters themselves. They also revealed the high standard of thought and interest that exists among the crew of one of H.M. ships in time of war. All the questions, of course, had to come from them.

The R.A.F. had a strong representation on the Brains Trust, the members including a Squadron Leader, a Corporal (described as " a student before the war ") and two other R.A.F. men. A young sailor rating, who was another member, was said to have been a zoologist before entering the Navy.

Before we had gone very far I was glad of the presence of the zoologist. A question on the Darwinian Theory led to all eyes being turned on him. He stepped in gallantly and most of us felt the situation was saved. Another question on the motive force of mother-love left me rather breathless, but Standing led on to a broad plane of discussion which gave everybody a chance to join in, even the poor shadow of Commander Campbell.

Everyone let himself go on the question : " What effect have the Services on one's mental development ? " There was a division of opinion, with the majority of the service personnel taking the view that development of the mind was not aided by months or years in the services, while I, for one, expressed the view that contacts and experiences might come to a man while in the services which he might not otherwise have had and which would certainly help to broaden his mental outlook.

Then there was the question of whether indiscriminate reading should be encouraged. This, too, as far as I remember, referred to men and women in the services who might read a lot of trash if they found themselves with considerable time on hand and little to occupy it. Would it be better to cut down their available reading matter rather than permit them to " soak " in third-rate books or novels ?

Again the answers were varied. One view was that there were service jobs which justified any sort of reading, provided it offered relaxation from the dull everyday routine. At the other extreme there was the opinion that three-quarters of all reading matter available to the services should be burnt at once.

The Question Master kept a sharp eye on his team and if an argument threatened to overwhelm the microphone he at once stepped in with a quietly decisive word and invariably rounded off the answers to each question with a neat summary.

All his tact was required when the *Hilary's* Brains Trust was asked whether it believed in euthanasia for mental and physical deficients. It was a subject on which surprisingly strong views were held by the small cross-section of people who faced the microphone. The matter was discussed in rather broader terms than the questioner had intended and, after the Brains Trust session had ended, it was being pursued in the ward-room.

A young doctor, only recently appointed to the ship, indicated the difficulties that would arise in framing laws to govern the whole subject. Tremendous responsibility would fall on the medical man. Making a comparison with the law as it stands in relation to abortion, he mentioned a case where a doctor had had to run the risk of very serious consequences for himself because he decided that an operation was justified in the case of a woman who was going to have a baby as the result of rape. Doctors were human beings and felt strongly on these matters. Was it fair that they should not only have to make grave decisions but, on occasions, risk their freedom in order to act as any humanitarian would wish to act ? If euthanasia were accepted, then the law should provide an authority to make decisions on the reports of doctors, rather than leave a considerable amount of the final responsibility on the shoulders of the doctors themselves. He pointed out that it was a heavy burden for the individual to carry when that individual knew that the developments of medical science might give a chance of cure to a case which, at the time the decision was called for, seemed incurable.

And in such discussions we passed the evening when but for the unexpected break in the weather, we should have been on the way to France with the Armies of Liberation.

Next morning, Monday, June 5th, showed little improvement in the weather. From a staff officer I heard that reports of weather to come were not encouraging, and the urgency of the whole situation became apparent when he added : " Tides, the moon and many other considerations have been worked out to the last fraction, and if we do not move in three days the whole operation must be put off for a fortnight."

Such a postponement would have created enormous problems, and outstanding among them would have been the problem of security. Thousands of officers and men had been " briefed " for the invasion at this stage, and many of them were in small craft from which they would have to be disembarked if there were to be a long period of waiting.

For forty-eight hours before the decision was made to proceed with the operation those who were responsible for making it must have gone through a period of intense anxiety. Whether that was the case or not, news came to the ship that the Prime Minister was making a last rapid tour in the Southampton–Portsmouth area and that his cigar was held at a particularly jaunty angle.

Admiral Ramsay came on board the *Hilary* for a short time, and he, too, appeared quite cheerful. He mentioned that it was only with considerable difficulty that they had persuaded Mr. Churchill that he would be running undue risks if he crossed with the invasion fleets to watch the actual storming of the beaches.

A steady stream of aircraft passed over the mass of shipping during the morning, heading for France. There was still a strong wind blowing, however, and the sea was rough enough to make one feel that any flat-bottomed craft would have an unpleasant time in the Channel.

It certainly caused a big surprise when we heard, around midday, that " the party was on." The landing craft were heading out again in what appeared to be a never-ending procession, and this time, unless there was a last-minute alteration in plan, there was real business to be done.

There was elation in H.M.S. *Hilary*. Every man in the ship seemed to be repeating " It's on ! " We knew that we should not move for some hours, but everybody felt a great impatience to get on with it. The Canadian colonel, with some more of his staff, came on board. There was a sparkle in his eye which revealed that he, too, was elated, although his mouth was set in a hard line. In the next few hours he would be leading his men in the front line of the assault on Europe. They would succeed if it was humanly possible to do so, but a price would have to be paid, and it was not a moment to be treated lightly.

The huge anchorage of L.C.T.'s away towards the Hampshire shore began to empty as vessels went out by the score. They were due to make a speed of about five knots all the way across the Channel. They were in for a long and rough passage.

In order that the assault could take place soon after dawn the next morning, I was told that it had been necessary for the first of the little ships to leave at 9 A.M. that day. It seemed impossible, with so much movement going on during the hours of daylight, that an element of surprise could be obtained when the assault finally took place.

The minesweepers had already gone to work, although their main task of sweeping a channel thirty-three miles long, with the tide ebbing or flooding all the time, would come a little later.

If all went well H hour was fixed for 7.25 A.M. on June 6th. For the American task force, operating to the west, it was fifty minutes earlier. It would be light just after 5 A.M.

All through that afternoon more and more vessels headed for the open sea. The decks of the big landing ships were lined with men, and one thought of the mass of fighting vehicles in the holds of the L.S.T.'s. By the time they left, the smaller craft, carrying the assault groups, were well out in the Channel. Reports came back that they were standing up to the heavy weather conditions very well.

In one of these parties were the special tanks which were to wade ashore and fight from the beaches like miniature fortresses. Royal Marines manned some of them—the first time that Marines had fought in tanks.

There were other curious D Day loads such as the fifty " ducks " taken in H.M.S. *Northway*.

Hundreds of ships were on their way by the time the *Hilary* sailed at 6.30 P.M. Out in the Channel we felt the full force of the wind and could see the buffeting that was being taken by some small craft that were in company with us. A Royal Marine Commando unit was taking passage in them. Before darkness came it was possible to see many ships, but it was but a fraction of the number we had seen leave, and there were more coming from ports and harbours all along the coast. About the same time as we sailed a big force was setting off from the Thames estuary. They were due to come in with a follow-up wave of support troops.

Aircraft, with their new bold black and white stripe markings on their wings, flew over continually.

We knew that, apart from bombing, the assault would be begun from the air several hours before the first storming of the beaches. As the whole world now knows, it was the 6th British Airborne Division and the 101st American Airborne Division who opened the attack on the citadel of Europe soon after midnight on June 6th, 1944. The first paratroops went down more or less at the extremes of the Allied landing area, with the British east of the Caen Canal and the Americans in the Cherbourg peninsula. Following the paratroops came gliderborne troops.

The success of these efforts was one of the most spectacular events of that historic day. It was said to me later that so important was the attack of the British airborne troops, covering the whole of the flank of the invasion as it did, that it would have had to go on, even if fifty per cent. casualties had had to be faced. Actually, although the weather was anything but ideal for such an operation, the casualties in the initial stages were no more than two and a half per cent. of the personnel. Three hundred and sixty aircraft and 96 gliders were used, I was told.

After darkness, as the drone of aircraft engines was heard above the hum of the ship's engines, we pictured these magnificent picked troops passing high above us and waiting for the signal that would drop them from the skies into battle. We knew that many more aircraft would be on a similar course and that their loads would be death-dealing, but not human. Night fighters, too, were up, defending the airborne divisions. They were going in to shoot up the German flak batteries and put out the searchlights.

Before it was light we saw the red and orange reflections of huge fires started by the bombers. The coast of France was still not in sight, but the reflections rose and fell as the bombs went down.

In a very matter-of-fact way a senior R.A.F. officer had said to me some time earlier, " Our aim is to bring about a situation which will enable the Navy and Army to carry out this operation without effective interference from the German air force." After ten hours at sea without the sight of a German plane one felt that the word " effective " was a little unnecessary.

During the hours of darkness, while the armada of Allied ships approached the coast of France, our Air Forces had been " softening " the enemy. About 750 heavy bombers, led by the Pathfinders, had gone in to attack the whole front. A special force had been detailed to bomb certain heavy batteries which the Germans were known to have in the region.

The attack of the heavies finished two hours before H hour and then the medium bombers followed, their selected targets being coast defence batteries.

It had been a long-drawn-out and effective softening— as we heard later from French people who spent that night in their air-raid shelters—but much more was to come.

Even as we picked out the first dim outline of the French coast—a flicker of flame from a fire on the land

first proved to us that we were actually looking at the
invasion beaches—another fleet of bombers roared overhead. These were the Fortresses and Liberators of the
8th and 9th Air forces going in to carry out the most con-
centrated air attack of all. Between H minus 30 and
H hour they were going to pulverise the coastal strip
with 1,900 tons of bombs on the American beaches and
2,400 tons on the British beaches. They had the close
support of fighter-bombers.

The complete absence of enemy aircraft was surprising,
because the estimated strength of the Lutfwaffe on the
Western Front just prior to D Day was 2,350 aircraft.
The British and American figure was over 10,000 but we
had considerable distances to fly from British airfields,
and in any case the need of the enemy coastal defenders
for some sort of air support was indeed desperate. The
distances that our aircraft were required to fly in order
to operate over the Normandy beaches had the most
pronounced effect in cutting down the operational time
of the fighters. Until we obtained landing strips in
France, I believe it was necessary to maintain ten fighter
squadrons in the south of England in order that one
should be continually over the assault area on the other
side of the Channel.

Many of the Navy men I talked to during the minus
hours of D Day and subsequently gave heartfelt praise
to the Allied air forces. They had had experience earlier
in the war of important operations which had to be
undertaken with little or no air support. To be free of
whistling bombs as they went about their business in the
most important operation of all surprised and delighted
them. It was almost too good to be true.

All through the hours of our approach to France,
fighter cover was provided, and the fact that the Germans
did not attempt to attack our shipping in the Channel
must have led to a lot of disappointed men flying back
to England.

In the *Hilary* most of the Canadian officers had snatched
an hour or two of sleep, but everybody was on the move

long before dawn. The headquarters ship had entered the swept Channel just as it was getting dark, and it was fascinating to stand on deck some hours later and pick out the dan buoys laid at regular intervals to mark the straight course of the sweepers. A small light glimmered from each buoy and they marked the Channel on both sides. This led a naval officer to remark, " It is as good as going down Oxford Street in peace-time." The lights were not as bright as all that, but they certainly appeared with the regularity of street lamp-posts.

Sweeping the channel that we followed were eight fleet minesweepers. They swept one behind the other in a long diagonal line so that the second sweeper came just within the area swept by the first, and so on right down the line. Two M.L.'s, right in the van, swept a course for the first sweeper.

Behind the first and last sweepers came the dan-laying ships. There were four altogether, two acting as reserves in case the first dan-layer in each line failed to get a buoy away, or dropped an unlighted buoy. One of the reserve dan-layers, I heard later, went all the way to France outside the swept channel rather than risk inter-fering with the vital work in hand.

Other channels were being swept further to the west for the Americans, the sweepers including the Canadian flotilla which had only recently crossed the Atlantic after doing many months of useful escort work on the other side.

The dan buoys still marked the swept channel after daylight came, and continued to within a mile or so of the French coast. It was only when the water became too shallow for the fleet sweepers to go on that they turned from their course and swept east and west in the anchorage area. Having carried out their duties with a devotion which was recognised as being of the highest possible standard even by the Navy—that service where the accepted standard is the best a man can do— the minesweepers modestly tucked themselves away where they would not interfere with the mass of shipping coming in behind them.

" We went and had a good sleep on top of a minefield which we were not required to sweep," was the way an officer put it to me when I went on board one of the sweepers a few days later.

IV

DAY OF DESTINY

*The day shall come, the great
avenging day . . . .*

ALEXANDER POPE.

AN L.C.T. ARRIVES ON THE NORMANDY BEACHES
(Royal Canadian Navy Photograph)

FIRES RAGE IN ST. BERNIERES-SUR-MER AS TROOPS POUR ASHORE

(Royal Canadian Navy Photograph)

CHAPTER IV

DAY OF DESTINY

ONLY a few hours earlier men of the *Hilary* had been gathered around the piano in their ward-room singing their own particular chorus :

> " All over the place
> The *Hilary* goes,
> To fight all our foes,
> To deal knock-out blows—
> That Jerry well knows,
> All over the place."

But in the first light of dawn on June 6th, 1944, there was a big change. A long table close to the piano was loaded with medical gear and the curtain near our temporary sleeping quarters had been pulled round to make a casualty station. Sick bay attendants sat by the piano, waiting.

At that moment we knew that the Second Front had opened. The Airborne Division was already fighting on French soil and Allied aircraft and warships were giving the final pounding to the chosen piece of coast.

We remembered the parting words of Admiral Ramsay as he left the *Hilary*. They were meant for every man in this unprecedented force : " Good luck—good luck to you all."

Certainly the luck had been with us so far. With the French coast looming ever clearer, we had overcome weather conditions such as had never even been considered when the plans for the assault were prepared. The sweep had been most successful and the whole invasion force had arrived off the Normandy coast with practically no losses.

But the hardest task of all still had to be faced—the

direct assault on the beaches. To what extent would the German first-line defences have survived the air-sea bombardment and how effective would their static defences still be, were the questions in our minds.

Six weeks earlier our Russian ally had examined these crucial matters in an article published in the Soviet journal, " War and the Working Class." It has been said that the Russians have found it hard to understand the complex nature of a huge land-sea operation. That may be the case, although there is plenty of evidence to the contrary, and I have no doubt that much of their insistence on the need for an early opening of yet another front by the other Allies was intended as a constant reminder to the Germans that the danger in the west was an ever-present one.

Within an hour or so of H hour, as we were, one's mind was vividly at work. A whole procession of thoughts flashed by, linked only by the significance of the moment. I could only vaguely recall the points of the Soviet article, but the thoughts were reassuring because, in some way, there was the feeling that, great land fighters as they are, the Russians could be expected to offer an expert but detached appreciation of D Day prospects.

These are the words I tried to remember : " The opening stage of the hostilities in Europe may be a landing operation on a strategic scale which the Allies hope will effectively bring the invasion armies to the Continent. What are the requisites for the performance of this operation ? The success of landing operations hinges first of all on possession of adequate land, sea and air forces and the quality of their training, and also on skilful and efficient co-ordination between the Navy, aircraft and ground troops. . . . The personnel of the invasion armies has long been undergoing training at the combined operations training base. We need only recall the highly successful operations of the Anglo-American troops in North Africa, Sicily, Sardina, Corsica, Italy and the Pacific Islands. It may be said without exaggera-

tion that the Allied store of experience in operations of
this kind is very great indeed, and it has been speedily
assimilated and followed in the training of the invasion
troops. But there are also some other very important
factors. To ensure a successful landing it is essential
to have sea and air supremacy, and for the Navy to have
at its disposal large numbers of special landing craft
and of transport vessels which will be able to bring up
speedily to the landing spot reinforcements and supplies
that will follow."

The article went on to examine these points in detail
and, on the naval side, came to the general conclusion
that, " In spite of losses, the fighting strength of the
British and American Navies—far from declining—has
grown considerably since the war began. The fact of
particular importance is the increase in the number of
vessels which can be employed to safeguard landing forces
against the action of mines and against air and submarine
attacks. . . . The Allies enjoy supremacy at sea as
regards both naval fire power and the means of safeguarding the crossing and landing of a large body of
troops."

" The second vital condition for safeguarding landing
operations is supremacy in the air," the Soviet writer
continued. " In modern landing operations it is essential
not only to provide air cover while the assault forces are
crossing, but to have secure air supremacy over the area
throughout. The air forces must form an air umbrella
over the landing troops, to enable them to fight successfully for the bridgehead. The Allied landing operation
at Nettuno was covered from the air by 900 fighter planes.
Quite apart from any accurate figures of British and
American airplanes, an analysis of some of the big recent
landing operations and air attacks on Germany leads
one to the unquestionable conclusion that our Allies' air-
power is sufficient for supremacy in the air in any operations undertaken, and particularly over the Channel area
and the coast of North-Western Europe."

At the moment when these matters were to be put to

the proof it was reassuring to recall the faith expressed in us by our other great ally. I, too, had a very full faith in our powers, but nothing is certain in this world until it has come to pass.

The first landing was being made by the American troops away to our right. They were due ashore before 7 A.M. The Canadians, with whom we were chiefly concerned as a headquarters ship, went in next and the two British frontal assaults followed closely after. In each case the troops had to storm over beaches and dunes or hills, beyond which the Germans had had years to prepare their defences.

The naval bombardment was in full swing. In its early stages it was most impressive away to the west, where the land curved seaward towards Cherbourg. The American warships were challenging any German gun that dared to speak and many more that had been silenced temporarily or permanently by the bombing from the air. The yellow flashes of the naval guns were accompanied by an almost unbroken roar of explosions.

Around us were dozens of landing craft, the men in them watching the blaze of gunfire or looking at the fleets of aircraft overhead. They cheered the planes, well knowing what this air supremacy meant to them. Spitfires raced across the sky, providing low cover over the assault area, while Thunderbolts of the 9th U.S. Air force twinkled almost out of sight as the high cover over the same area.

British Hunt-class destroyers, going boldly for the shore, engaged enemy gun positions at point-blank range. It was an indication to us that we had reached H minus 40. In little more than half an hour the Canadians would be over the beaches.

The final terrific attack on the beach defences was delivered by the rocket-firing craft. They went in with their barrel-like guides pointing ahead, but carefully angled, so that when they fired the destructive rockets went out as if they had been discharged from a giant spray. It is hard to comprehend the awful effect of

68

this one form of attack. The rocket craft put down thousands of rounds of rockets on each of four beaches in half an hour.

All along the beaches fortress tanks moved in and then sat down solidly and engaged any enemy pillbox or forward post which still sought to stand in the path of the invading infantry.

From the *Hilary*, still some three miles out at sea, it was possible to observe a large section of the beach. The spires of the churches in Bernieres-sur-mer and Courseuilles had been landmarks for our approach. Away on the left towards Ouistreham a particularly large fire was raging. It had acted like a beacon for more than an hour, first blazing up fiercely and then dying away for a time, only to break out in another mass of sweeping flames.

Suddenly one was conscious of a silence. There was still the endless drone of aircraft, the noise of the engines of small craft round about us and the light rattle of fire from the shore. But it was " silence " in comparison with the period when the naval guns were pounding the enemy. The bombardment from the ships had come to an end temporarily. Later it would be resumed on targets chosen by the Army as they pressed inland.

First reports arriving in the headquarters ship told of the success of the British Airborne Division in their landings to the east of the Caen canal. Not only had they gained the high ground they were sent in to capture, but they had struck with such speed that important bridges, which it was thought the Germans would have ample time to destroy, had been captured intact.

Now the main assault was on, and in two and a half hours the whole of the initial assault force, with all their supporting arms, including the bridging companies, would be in.

There was still no sign of the Luftwaffe, and practically all opposition from enemy guns on shore had ceased. We had been warned that German heavy guns flanking our landing area from the direction of Le Havre would

be able to drop shells into the fleet of invasion ships
and on to the beaches, if they survived a major air
attack and, if necessary, sea bombardment. The shells
did not arrive, so one concluded, not without relief, that
once again air and sea supremacy had triumphed.

Hundreds of landing craft could be seen spread out all
along the beaches. Some, indeed, were already heading
out to seaward again. They passed others going in. The
bigger landing ships were there, ready to disgorge their
masses of men and tanks and guns right on to French
soil.

Flying very high, so high that they could not be seen
with the naked eyes, the day bombers, Fortresses and
Liberators, droned over in ear-strumming bulk. Small
craft began to appear from nowhere, skimming among the
larger ships like so many anxious ducklings.

One came alongside the *Hilary* and, with a slight shock
one realised that it carried the first grim proof of the
fact that, even with air and sea supremacy, frontal
attacks on strongly-prepared positions cannot be carried
out without loss. Some wounded men, both soldiers and
sailors, were helped on board. A few had to be hauled
up in cradles. One was found to be already dead ; another
died soon afterwards, lying close to my bed in the little
temporary sick bay of the *Hilary*. We hoped they had
lived long enough to know that they had taken part in
the greatest and most wonderfully successful operation
of the whole war.

" The greatest amphibious operation in history " was
the description of Admiral Ramsay. To all naval men
taking part in the invasion, the Naval Commander-in-
Chief of the Allied Expeditionary Force had issued the
following Order of the Day : " It is to be our privilege
to take part in the greatest amphibious operation in
history—a necessary preliminary to the opening of the
Western Front in Europe which, in conjunction with the
great Russian advance, will crush the fighting power of
Germany. This is the opportunity which we have long
awaited and which must be seized and pursued with

relentless determination ; the hopes and prayers of the free world and of the enslaved people of Europe will be with us, and we cannot fail them. Our task, in conjunction with the Merchant Navies of the United Nations and supported by the Allied Air Forces, is to carry the Allied Expeditionary Force to the Continent, to establish there a secure bridgehead, and to build it up and maintain it at a rate which will outmatch that of the enemy. Let no one underestimate the magnitude of this task. The Germans are desperate, and will resist fiercely until we outmanœuvre and outfight them, which we can and we will do. To everyone of you will be given the opportunity to show by his determination and resource that dauntless spirit of resolution which individually strengthens and inspires and which collectively is irresistible. I count on every man to do his utmost to ensure the success of this great enterprise, which is the climax of the European war. Good luck to you all and God-speed."

· For the Canadian Naval units there was added this special message from Vice-Admiral Percy W. Nelles, Senior Canadian Flag Officer Overseas: " I very much regret not being with you now or during the eventful days ahead, days which will live for ever in the history of mankind. I am confident of your success, for you are Canadians and know for what you are all fighting. I am also confident in you as members of the Canadian Navy and feel sure, although the struggle ahead will be bitter, that Canada will have very good reason to be proud of her Navy in this our greatest test, as she was proud of our part in beating the U-boats in the Atlantic. Good luck, good fighting, and speedy victory to you all."

Rear-Admiral A. G. Kirk, U.S.N., in command of the Western naval task force, had said earlier, in disclosing to a party of war correspondents where the invasion would take place, " I have no doubt we will put them ashore," and had added that supplies would continue to go in by sea after D Day until Germany was beaten.

The naval forces thus addressed numbered more officers

and men than the total personnel of the Royal Navy at the commencement of the war.

The minesweepers alone numbered about two hundred and they were manned by ten thousand officers and men. The weight of the minesweeping gear they had to handle approached three thousand tons, and their sweep wires, joined end to end, would have reached from London to the Isle of Wight.

Only the long and patient studies of the historian will provide anything like the full story of the way Allied naval men rose to the call of D Day. Here I can do no more than record a few individual cases of the heroism shown all along the beaches in the early phases of the great assault.

The first American infantrymen, following their tanks, climbed up their section of the beach at 0633, as the official documents say—in other words, 6.33 a.m. Heavier waves followed after the demolition units had made a path through the obstacles. There was a strong wind which made the sea quite rough, but the landing craft pressed on, although a few were capsized when they got close in.

The assault landing craft were among the smallest of the vessels going in to the beaches. One flotilla, manned by Royal Navy personnel, carried soldiers of the 5th United States Rangers (the American Commando formations). For the last fifty yards of their journey the craft had to manœuvre between the maze of obstacles just off the beach. Practically all of these obstacles had mines or shells attached to them, and one collision would have been sufficient to blow these little boats out of the water. There was still heavy machine-gun and mortar fire coming across the beach—no doubt some of the Germans had returned to their weapons from the deep concrete shelters in which they managed to escape the bombing and bombardment from the warships. Senior Officer of the Flotilla was Lieut. E. H. West, R.N.V.R., and every craft under his command reached the beach. The Rangers scrambled out into less than two feet of

water. In his report subsequently Lieut. West wrote :
" I must say that after a very rough passage and a certain
amount of sea-sickness, the Rangers went ashore in
exceptionally good spirits."

In the short time that the soldiers and sailors were
together a fine comradeship sprang up between them.
I personally heard of instances of Navy men dashing
up the beaches after the soldiers they had brought in
in order to give them a last handshake and wish them
good luck.

Another of the small craft launched from a parent ship
was swamped on the way in. The Commanding Officer,
Lieut. T. H. B. Woodhouse, R.N.V.R., a London man,
was left swimming in the water with the rest of his
crew and the soldiers who had been taking passage.
Another officer in the flotilla, Sub-Lieut. T. S. Carrick,
has described what happened : " We struck a particularly
bad patch of sea. Many of the American infantrymen
we were taking in were sick. There was a danger of
our being swamped, so I reduced speed. Even then we
had to keep the pump going and soldiers were baling.
About two miles away from the parent ship, Lieut.
Woodhouse's craft broke formation. I thought he was
dodging a mine until I saw his bows well down and the
crew and infantrymen jumping into the water. After
the craft sank, Lieut. Woodhouse appeared to be sitting
in the water taking things calmly until someone came
to his assistance. It looked as though he had been doing
that sort of thing all his life. Lieut. Woodhouse was
picked up by another landing craft and promptly resumed
command of the flotilla."

Another craft which came to grief, but in this case
not until the job was well and truly done, was that
commanded by Lieut. N. Fraser, R.N.V.R. Later Lieut.
Fraser reported : " The combination of head-sea and
tidal race was too much for her, and she flooded forward.
After about five minutes her screws were almost clear
of the water and she became unmanageable. Six of the
crew were swept overboard and almost immediately a

light machine-gun in the cliffs opened up on them. A rapid reply from our guns stopped this fire and we pulled our men inboard. Just as we were getting the last man in, a heavier weapon opened up on us and hit the craft in three places aft. This gun, and the light machine-gun supporting it, were at once engaged, and after a thousand round from us lost all further interest. By keeping all the crew on the shoreward side lying flat on deck, danger from odd rounds of fire was reduced, although hits were taken on the after compartment, the engine-room and the upper deck."

In spite of her perilous condition, this craft refused an offer to be taken in tow and went on doing her job until she could do it no more. After about four hours, when she had all but sunk, an M.L. took off her crew. It was not until that moment that Engineer Leading Stoker Atkinson left the little engine room where he had kept the engines going throughout.

The " determination and resource " asked for by the Naval Commander-in-Chief was displayed to the full by a nineteen-year-old Royal Marine corporal, who was subsequently awarded the Distinguished Service Medal. Corporal G. E. Tandy used to be an auto-machinist in south-east London. On D Day it was his duty as a newly-promoted corporal, Royal Marines, to act as Coxswain of Assault Craft No. 786, which was launched from its parent ship seven miles from the Normandy coast. When the time came to launch the little vessel there was a high sea running. As she bobbed up and down in the water the heavy hook on which she had been suspended as she dropped into the water smashed down on the steering wheel and shattered the engine-room telegraph. Normally it would have been possible to steer the craft by her engines but the swell was too great for that.

Describing what happened then, Lieut.-Commander H. Wheeler, of the parent ship, said : " Tandy, like all of us, realised how essential it was that every soldier should be landed on the enemy beach if it were humanly possible.

He was not to be beaten by what seemed to be an impossible situation. He slipped over the square stern, placed one foot on the rudder guard-rail, and directly controlled the rudder with his other foot. He had only the shallow rim of wood round the stern of the boat and a little iron cleat to hang on to. In this way he faced a seven-miles journey to the French shore. How he hung on was a miracle. At one moment he was high out of the water and the next he was plunged back in the sea up to his arm-pits. How his leg was not broken against the rudder rail was a mystery. Shouting orders to the stoker coaxing the engine, Tandy steered the craft right in to the beaches. Close in he had to guide the craft between stakes and girders, many of them with teller mines attached to them. The craft was also under fire."

L.C.A. 786 arrived exactly where she was scheduled to go and only three minutes behind the time laid down.

But even then Tandy did not consider that his duty had been done to the full. He decided that he would hang on for another seven miles and get his boat back from the Normandy beaches to the parent ship. He faced an even greater ordeal because, on the return journey, the wind and seas were against the little craft. After two hours and forty-five minutes on this outward journey, Corporal Tandy brought L.C.A. 786 alongside her parent ship. He was hauled out of the water, his body numbed and bruised by the long buffeting in the sea. After two days in the sick bay of the ship, all he had to say about his action was : " There were thirty-two soldiers' lives at stake in that boat, sir, apart from the sailors manning her. Any one of them would have done the same as I did if they had had the opportunity."

My friend Commander Peter MacRitchie, R.C.N.V.R., who took passage in one of the landing craft, has given a graphic description of how Canadian Navy units helped to land the crack Canadian troops. " One of the two landing craft (infantry) flotillas, was circling in a wide sweep off-shore waiting for orders to beach," he wrote.

" I had sailed across in a craft commanded by Lieut. Hugh McColl Harrison, R.C.N.V.R., of Toronto. We had started out from a British port early in the afternoon of the previous day, after having made one false start when D Day had to be postponed for twenty-four hours. Three hours after the first landing had been effected, the order to beach came to the Canadians in a most dramatic way. The signal said, in effect : ' Assault landing craft having a hard time. Will you have a go, Canada ? ' There was a mere acknowledgment from Lieut.-Commander H. T. Huston, R.C.N.V.R., of Rossburn, Manitoba, the flotilla officer. Then, with the beaches ablaze, the twelve Canadian craft assigned to this particular beach spun around and, like thoroughbreds prancing to the starting-gate, were off. They surged through the surf at full speed, the troops in the craft holding tight to the stanchions. In a trice they had crashed their way on to the sand, the ramps were down and, led by a piper playing his regimental march, the soldiers were wading ashore with rifles and bicycles held high over their heads. Mines and other Nazi devices were exploding at second intervals under the ships, but in the entire flotilla there was only one casualty, a signalman, who suffered slight shrapnel wounds."

" When the troops reached shore " (the account continued), " they undertook a job which was different from that which the pre-invasion plans had called for. This unit was a follow-up unit and the men were supposed to leap on their bicycles and force their way inland up to a certain spot, and there dig in. But as we reached the beach, we could see that it was not being held by Allied troops. The unit was therefore obliged to create a bridgehead until such time as another unit moved in to take over this part of the operation. Then they moved inland on their bicycles to take up the task to which they had been originally detailed. Further along to the eastward another flotilla, under Lieut.-Commander Hugh Doheny, R.C.N.V.R., of Montreal, was doing equally effective work with its portion of the unit, while yet another flotilla, under Lieut.-Commander L. S. Kyle, R.C.N.V.R., of Vancouver, was teaming-up with the United States Navy in beaching troops of another force."

As the landing force went in Commander MacRitchie saw the two Canadian destroyers *Algonquin* (Lieut.-Commander D. W. Piers, D.S.C., R.C.N.) and *Sioux* (Lieut.-Commander Eric Boak, R.C.N.) firing on the inshore batteries, and the two Canadian L.C.A. parent ships, *Prince Henry* (Captain V. S. Godfrey, R.C.N.) and *Prince David* (Commander T. D. Kelly, R.C.N.R.) were also there.

The Canadian Navy men who landed their own country-men in France on D Day promised to be waiting for the soldiers when they had cleaned up and were ready to go back to Canada. Most of the soldiers had had enough of small craft, however, and declined the offer, with thanks.

It goes without saying that all the British Dominions were represented on this day, and in giving these cameos of personal exploits I would mention a South African, Lieut. J. E. Ramsay, S.A.N.F., of Durban. Four months before the outbreak of war he came to this country for training with the Royal Navy. By the end of 1943, and while still in his early twenties, he had completed twenty-five thousand miles at sea.

On the eve of D Day he found himself in command of a small naval vessel engaged with the advance force of minesweepers. On the way to France he swept a number of mines and actually arrived on the other side of the Channel before it was completely dark on the evening of June 5th. Early next morning a Ju 88 appeared, and Lieut. Ramsay's vessel, opening fire, had the satisfaction of securing what was probably the first " bag " of D Day.

Next, Lieut. Ramsay came upon a small freighter which had been damaged and was in danger of sinking. It was packed with troops, and a destroyer was standing by with its scrambler nets down, ready to pick up the men. But heavy seas were running and there was the danger that some men might get swept away or that

77

the two ships might crash together and crush the soldiers as they clambered on the nets. Lieut. Ramsay nosed his vessel between the destroyer and the freighter and so acted as a buffer to keep them steady while the men passed from one to the other.

One further adventure befell the young South African. Unable to find a senior British officer to report to, he went to a United States ship. An American officer, putting his head out of a scuttle, inquired, " Can I help you, Lieutenant ? " " I expect so," said Ramsay, and was invited to the U.S. officer's cabin. He found himself face to face with Admiral Hall, U.S.N., who was commanding the naval task force in that area.

An even younger D Day hero was Midshipman Charles Fowler, of Liverpool, who, at nineteen, was First Lieut. of a tank landing craft. As the vessel ran into the beaches it came under heavy fire from Germans hiding in a house close to the shore. The guns of the L.C.T. replied, but one gun suddenly jammed. The Commanding Officer rushed from the bridge to aid the gunner, but was mortally wounded before he reached the gun. Midshipman Fowler took command of the craft and carried on although her steering gear was shot away. In the face of continued heavy fire she unloaded her tanks. A mortar bomb landed on the deck of the L.C.T., but before it could explode Leading Stoker J. Gamble, of Colne, Lincolnshire, seized it and threw it back at the enemy. It exploded among a nest of Germans. The casualties in the L.C.T. were mounting—two of the crew were killed and three wounded—but Midshipman Fowler finished the unloading of his craft and then found that she was stuck on the sands. He went ashore to get assistance and managed to persuade the driver of an army bulldozer to help them off with a shove and a heave of his powerful vehicle. There was still a strong wind blowing, the sea was rough, and the lightly-built landing craft had no steering gear working. Undaunted, Midshipman Fowler, who had never before had command of a vessel, headed the craft for England. Steering with his engines, he reached the south coast some hours later.

The crew of another L.C.T. spent ten hours on the beach, after getting their passengers ashore, trying to salvage their damaged craft. Commanded by Sub-Lieut. Ernest Mills, R.N.V.R., of Nuneaton, the craft was damaged in the bows by a tank as she ran on to the beaches. Worse trouble followed when a jeep fell into deep water and blocked the way for the other vehicles that had to be unloaded.

Sub-Lieut. Mills, under sporadic enemy shelling, allowed his vessel to drift to another part of the beach and unloading was resumed. Shortly after, another craft, which had been hit by a shell, drifted on to the L.C.T. and carried away her kedge line. Sub-Lieut. Mills found that the only way to keep his vessel in contact with the beach was to keep both engines driving slowly forward. When the port engine seized, they still managed to maintain the boat in position on the starboard engine alone, but, under the double strain, that also failed after three-quarters of an hour.

Unloading had not been completed, so the young Commanding Officer allowed the L.C.T. to drift broadside on on to the beach, although he knew that it would give them little chance of getting off again when their main task was finished. Shells continued to arrive on the beach and one hit the ward room of the L.C.T. Nobody had time to spend in the ward-room, so there were no casualties. Efforts to salvage the craft were continued until evening, but it was impossible until the proper gear was available, so the plucky crew was taken off by another vessel and returned to England.

These are just a few examples of the brand of courage displayed by the Navy men who had the responsibility of delivering the army on D Day, a day of foul weather and many trials for the seaman quite apart from anything the Germans could provide. But, in the words of Anthony Trollope : " It's dogged as does it. It ain't thinking about it."

LANDING CRAFT IN THE QUEUE FOR THE BEACHES

(Royal Canadian Navy Photograph)

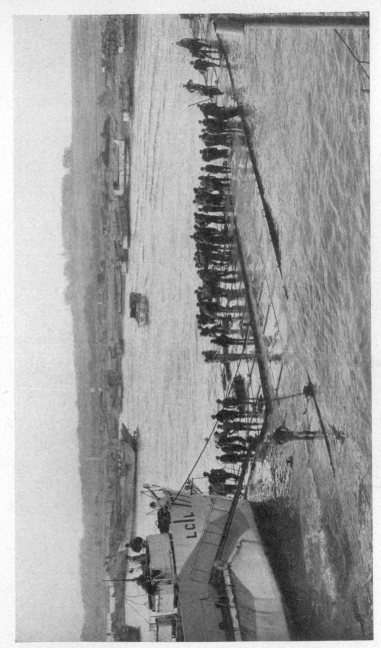

A " DE LUXE " LANDING ON A FLOATING JETTY FOR MEN FROM L.C.I.

(Royal Canadian Navy Photograph)

V

THE THUNDER OF ASSAULT

*They that go down to the sea in ships,
that do business in great waters; these
see the works of the Lord and His wonders
in the deep.*

PSALM 107.

V

THE THUNDER OF ASSAULT

IT was only natural that the thoughts of the men engaged in this vast operation should slip back occasionally over the hundred miles of sea to England and that they should say, with a grin, " This will shake them up a bit at home ! "

Actually the Navy had fulfilled the greater part of its obligations in regard to the initial landings before England and the rest of the world knew that it was D Day.

Shortly before 7 a.m. there was a German broadcast that said : " Early this morning numerous landing craft and light warships were observed in the area between the mouth of the Seine and the eastern coast of Normandy. . . . The harbour of Le Havre is at the moment being bombarded. German naval forces have engaged enemy landing craft off the coast."

The truth provides an amusing sidelight on the latter statement. The only German naval forces to become involved in D Day activities were some light craft that rushed out of Le Havre when word came that small British vessels were approaching. In the early morning light these dashing enemy naval units sighted more and more ships heading into the bay of the Seine. They may even have seen the *Rodney* with her mighty 16-inch turrets. What is certain, however, is that " the German naval forces " turned about and went back to Le Havre even faster that they came out.

A communique issued from Allied Supreme headquarters at 9.30 a.m. was the first official announcement in Britain of the invasion. Later in the morning Mr. Churchill was able to tell the House of Commons that an immense armada of more than 4,000 ships, with several thousand smaller craft, had crossed the Channel. " The landings on the beaches are proceeding at various points at the present time," he said. "The fire of the shore batteries has been largely quelled. The obstacles which were constructed in the sea have not proved so difficult as was apprehended."

"This vast operation is undoubtedly the most complicated and difficult that has ever occurred," the Prime Minister added. "There are already hopes that actual tactical surprise has been attained, and we hope to furnish the enemy with a succession of surprises during the course of the fighting."

There is no doubt that Mr. Churchill was right in declaring that, although it was inevitable that the Germans should know of our gigantic preparations for invasion, we did, at the last moment, achieve a measure of surprise. It is possible that the Germans were lulled into a false sense of security by the bad weather conditions. It may be, too, that those same conditions interfered with their own reconnaissance. Enemy E boats were said to have been out in the Channel every night except the actual night on which we sailed for France.

The landings had undoubtedly sounded an "Alert" in Europe and General Eisenhower had made no overstatement when in his Order of the Day to the assault forces, he said, "The eyes of the world are upon you. The hopes and prayers of liberty-loving people everywhere march with you."

Ships were still going in and troops were still running over the beaches when men, women and children all over the world were kneeling in silent prayer. To Europe, the Allied Supreme Commander broadcast the wonderful news : "This landing is part of the concerted United Nations' plan for the liberation of Europe, made in conjunction with our great Russian allies. I have this message for all of you. Although the initial assault may not have been made in your own country, the hour of liberation is approaching."

And while the news was told to the world the men in the fighting found ways and means of passing the news around among themselves. The radio broadcasts gave

them a much better knowledge of what was going on
than would have been possible in other wars. One ship,
H.M.C.S. *Prince David* actually produced a special invasion edition of " The David Prints." In duplicated
typescript the editorial stated : " To commemorate this
eventful week, the staff of ' The David Prints ' has
arranged to run a full eye-witness account of the operation."

This remarkable news sheet certainly kept its word.
Here are some extracts from its first-hand report :
" H.M.C.S. *Prince David* landed her first body of invasion troops exactly on schedule on the beach at Bernieres-sur-mer. The soldiers, members of a French-
Canadian regiment recruited from the lower St. Lawrence,
were ferried from the parent ship by the landing craft
flotillas, commanded by Lieut. R. G. Buckingham. It
was not until the assault infantry and tank landing
craft were practically on the beach that they ran into
trouble in the form of mines. The small assault boats
were the heaviest sufferers. Lieut. J. F. Beveridge was
the only naval casualty. He was cut on the head and
leg but his wounds were not serious. Bernieres-sur-mer
was a shambles as the boats came in. A dozen great
fires were burning and clouds of smoke rolled down the
beach. Every house gaped with shell-holes and there
were large rents in the village church steeple. The boats
rode in with a stiff wind that sent the surf crashing on the
beach. Their way lay through a section of crossed
scantlings which gave this piece of water the appearance
of a field filled with stumps. These were the mine
supports. First Lieut. J. McBeath's boat was mined,
then Lieut. Buckingham, Lieut. Beveridge and Leading
Seaman G. Lavergne had their craft smashed by other
mines. It was a wild scramble for shore, but everyone
made it, with the exception of two French-Canadians in
Lieut. McBeath's boat. They were killed outright by
the mine which their boat hit. While our boats were
emptying their men, others were taking punishment
from mines further up the beach. Chunks of débris
rose a hundred feet in the air and troops, now hugging

the shelter of a breakwater, were peppered with pieces of wood. The bigger landing craft did not escape, but they could take it. There were six German prisoners sitting in a sombre row on the sands. They had been captured by the first wave of Canadian infantrymen. Our flotilla crews had hopes of getting back to the parent ship in their one surviving boat, commanded by Lieut. Don Graham, but this one was also lost. She ran foul of a steel mine support which stove a hole in her and she had to be abandoned. An R.N. tank landing craft brought our sailors back to the ship. The second wave of troops was moving off as they arrived."

The " David Prints " certainly had an eye-witness story and one which many journals with much wider circulations would have been glad to publish.

Soon after H hour H.M.S. *Hilary* moved in to a central position off Juno beach and it was possible to get a grandstand view of all that was going on inshore. More and more ships and craft continued to arrive and life spread across the beaches as the sappers cleared wider paths through the mines. There still remained large empty spaces on the sands which were more marked as the tide began to fall.

In the ships congregating in the anchorage all guns were manned and many eyes scanned the skies for enemy aircraft. Planes there were in plenty but the R.A.F. and the U.S. Air forces had the skies to themselves. During the morning more than 1,300 Fortresses and Liberators, with a powerful fighter escort, streamed over the invasion coast to blast enemy defences in an attack which lasted for two and a half hours. Another wave of bombers which arrived about midday did not unload all their bombs because heavy cloud made it difficult to be certain that they were clear of our own forces.

Reports flowed in to the operations room of H.M.S. *Hilary* and some of the aircraft were directly controlled from the former merchant ship lying off the beaches.

From the moment the first troops were ashore, the Canadian army officers and headquarters personnel aboard the *Hilary* were restless to be with the fighting soldiers. It was their duty, however, to control the assault forces from the ship and only move ashore when the first wave of battle had left the beaches behind. When the time came for them to go ashore these splendid Canadians, including War Correspondent Ross Munro, went off with positive pleasure.

" Chiefy," the ex-Merchant Navy Chief Steward, had proved once again that the men just behind the front line deserve to be ranked with the actual fighting men. Although he had the responsibility of feeding hundreds of men under most difficult circumstances this more than middle-aged warrant officer remained the best humoured man aboard, ready to act as universal provider at a moment's notice.

The bigger ships had resumed the bombardment of enemy positions. They were shooting-up strong points, concentrations of troops and artillery positions. The " drenching " of the beaches was already a thing of the past and the barrage had moved on to break down points of resistance further inland. Forward observation posts had been established to direct this fire. Air observers also played an important part and " Forward Observers Bombardment " directed the fire of individual bombarding ships and called for additional fire power from the Naval Commander when it was necessary.

The bay of the Seine presented a never-to-be-forgotten sight at this time. The traffic to the beaches continued but it was now doubled by the flow of empty craft coming away again. The latter were in such numbers as to testify to an enormous quantity of both troops and materials already being ashore. The support troops going in sat on top of their vehicles or leaned over the rails of the vessels, mostly gazing towards the shore where heavy columns of smoke still rose from the fires. Many of the craft passed close to the *Hilary* and I was surprised to find that hardly a man showed any outward signs of sea-sickness, although many of them must have been sufferers on the crossing. I recalled the words of an army officer, who was also an experienced sailor, on another occasion when the commandos were on passage, " They are ill now but as soon as there is any fighting to be done they will be as fit as fiddles."

It was still a scene of movement with ships of all shapes and sizes coming and going. The warships moved along the coast where the sweepers had cleared a wide area. They wore their battle ensigns and the stiff breeze made these stand out much as one would have expected them to in a magnificent painting. The White Ensign predominated because this was a British zone but there were also numerous Stars and Stripes to mark the unity of the two great nations on this historic occasion.

Away towards Le Havre huge flashes were to be seen coming from the guns of two big ships. They were, I believe, the battleship *Warspite* and the monitor *Roberts*. Their firing was unhurried but tremendously effective because it was possible to see the clouds of smoke go up from the bursting shells which must have been twelve or fifteen miles away.

Over the smaller ships in the anchorage a silver canopy of barrage balloons added to the scene. The beach was thickly lined with vessels, some of which were clearly left high and dry by the receding tide.

A cruiser opened fire near the *Hilary*, the flash of her guns giving a split-second warning of the ear-splitting crash to follow. The yellow cloud of cordite had hardly rolled away when there was another big flash of flame. She was firing, I learned a little later, at a dangerous heavy battery just over the hill to the east of Bernieres and quickly obtained five direct hits.

We had warning that there were some Heinkels and Me 109's about. Once they came in sight but were gone again so quickly with a batch of Spitfires on their tails that I failed to find them with my binoculars. News came that two of the Heinkels had been shot down.

Our own fighters passed over in a steady stream, their broad black and white markings being easily seen at a distance. It took a little time to realise that our air forces had almost complete supremacy in the air and, with so many ships about, it was inevitable that, here and there, there should be a gunner a little too ready to " let go." This applied mostly to the smaller ships where the system of aircraft recognition was not as highly developed as in the warships. But one man with a light trigger finger may start a whole bombardment and it soon became apparent that a tightening of control on all anti-aircraft fire was necessary.

Looking ahead a little from this time, it can be said that it became even more apparent after one or two nights had proved extremely noisy. The matter was dealt with for our Force by Commodore Oliver. I happened to be present when he was shown a signal which it was proposed to pass to all ships. The signal began : " No ship will open fire on an aircraft unless orders. . . ." The Commodore glanced at the signal and promptly simplified it by saying " Cut out all words after ' aircraft.' "

Occasionally wounded and survivors arrived in the *Hilary* during the early part of D Day. One party of Americans were survivors from a mined L.C.I. " Gee," they said, " it is kind of hard to have come all the way we have come and then get bumped on the run in."

There were also about forty American tank men who were brought in from their L.C.T. which had been tossing about in the Channel all night following an engine failure. They had had a very unpleasant time, their drifting craft being almost swamped on several occasions. They were grimy, wet and tired by the time they reached the *Hilary* but they had hung on to their smallarms and nobody was missing. " We ought to have been in the first wave," a sergeant told me regretfully.

A little later I saw one of these men sitting down with a big mug of hot tea and a " door-step " of bread and jam. It was the first food he had had for twenty-four hours but, even as he consumed it, he was busily cleaning a tommy-gun.

There was a big improvement in the weather during the afternoon. The sun broke through, bringing warmth and cheerfulness, which reflected our feelings, because the news had come that the Canadians had taken their first and second objectives and, at some points, were nearly seven miles inland.

Caen had been mentioned to me as a final objective for the British forces on D Day. As everyone knows, we reached the outskirts of the famous Normandy town within the first twenty-four hours but did not actually take it until much later. That was because the Germans saw fit to throw in a considerable proportion of the armour at their disposal in France in a desperate effort to prevent our taking Caen. They made it the hinge of their own defence system. Having done that, they had dictated the trend of events for the last time. Field Marshal Montgomery promptly pinned down the German armour while he swung open the door to France through the American sectors in the Cherbourg peninsula. As the United States armies raced through Brittany and swung in a wide arc towards Paris, Montgomery, who had faced the Germans in battle ever since the 1939–40 days of the B.E.F. in France, crushed the remnants of the enemy armour which had been engaged, in some of the most bloody battles of the war, by British and Canadian troops.

To us, watching the first support troops go in behind the assault, these things were glories yet to be unfolded.

At sundown on the first day there was a little procession from the *Hilary*. The bodies of the two naval men who had died earlier in the day were buried at sea. Wrapped in heavy canvas and weighted, they were taken away in one of the boats. Each body was covered with the White Ensign. The brief burial service was read by one of the ship's officers and then those who had made the great sacrifice slipped quietly to their last resting place.

Almost before the boat was back alongside, the first German bombs to come anywhere near the *Hilary* had dropped harmlessly into the sea. It was not a raid in force. Most of the day there had been enemy planes marked on the chart in the Operations room. In most cases they had been intercepted before getting any-

where near the anchorage but, occasionally, one or two
planes slipped in, unloaded their bombs, and scuttled off
with Spitfires after them. Four or five German aircraft,
I heard, had been shot down over the sea before they
could even regain land.

During the evening we watched the *Rodney* pass to her
anchorage not far from us. The great battleship moved very
slowly among the many vessels, her shrill warship siren
wailing a warning to any moving craft that got in her way.
Hundreds of men could be seen on her long forecastle and
manning the formidable number of anti-aircraft guns.

The appearance of these sailors would have surprised
many people. Hardly a man wore the traditional blue
rig—that is the British sailor's going ashore dress. He
fights in a much more casual *ensemble*, although before
going into action he is usually advised to put on clean
underclothing so as to avoid the chance of infection if he
suffers any wound. A vest, or white or blue jersey, with
an old pair of slacks and trimmings supplied by antiflash
hoods and gloves and an all-enveloping duffle coat if it is
cold, is battle rig for the majority of our sailors.

But, however they were dressed in the *Rodney*, we knew
that it would not affect their efficiency. As to the presence
of the great ship close to us, there were two schools of
thought in the *Hilary*. The less cheerful felt that she would
draw whatever planes the Germans had like moths to a
candle : the other school gloried in the collection of anti-
aircraft weapons which would be brought to bear on these
planes by the *Rodney*, should they pay a visit.

And so D Day drew to an end, with the whole long
beach alive with Allied soldiers and sailors—there was
work for the Navy, as well as the Army, on the foreshore.
The whole of the organisation of each beach was under
the control of a naval officer—the Beach Commander.
Having landed immediately after the first wave of assault
troops, it became his responsibility to see that each
specialised section, either of personnel or stores, found,
on landing, its right place in the beach area and did not
get in the way of those following.

"D Day" and "H Hour" will remain as living terms in the English language. There have been various suggestions as to their origin and it should not be difficult to settle the point in the future. I believe these markings of time, which were to concern millions, came naturally to the United States army. In the last war an American army field order stated that an attack would open at "H hour" on "D Day," the actual time and date being filled in subsequently.

A most elaborate system of sea defence had been arranged for the mass of Allied shipping in its anchorages at night off the Normandy coast. The whole area was divided into squares which were covered by an inner patrol of destroyers, corvettes and other warships. Outside, the anchorages were ringed by minesweepers and other vessels capable of giving a warm reception to any E or R boats attempting to enter the anchorages. Submarines, too, were provided for, although, from the beginning, the experts had discounted the idea that U-boats could be used close-in against our invasion shipping. Beyond these immediate defences there were the fast M.T.B. flotillas and widely flung destroyer screens, supported, if necessary, by cruisers.

Air attack at night was another problem, but the ships had the double defence of their own massed anti-aircraft weapons and the night fighter patrols provided by the Allied air forces.

It was from the air that the main enemy attack developed on the night of D Day. Almost before darkness fell, odd German planes began to appear over the shipping. They were also attempting to bomb the beaches and, as night came, the sky was lit with the tracer shells of our anti-aircraft guns. The ships put up a terrific cannonade which echoed through the *Hilary* as if a thousand riveters were actually at work on her hull.

The headquarters ship had a particularly hoarse siren, short blasts on which were the "air-raid warning" for the ships in the vicinity. A long blast was the "all clear." The siren seemed to be in almost continual use during the night, so that, after many alarms, one humorist, listening to the grating notes, declared, " This ship is more likely to die of thirst than be sunk by German bombs ! "

It was difficult to estimate the strength of the enemy attacks, but heavy thumps from time to time left no doubt that bombs were being dropped in the anchorage. A cool calculation was made by one naval officer of the odds against a ship being hit. Taking the over-all amount of water surface as against the actual surface provided by the decks of ships, the odds were very good indeed—but the argument was not convincing enough to permit many people to go to bed and sleep unconcernedly.

Daylight, which came before 5 A.M., brought a restful quietness to the anchorage. Several big fires had apparently been started on shore, but, as far as one could see, all the ships were just where they had been at dusk the previous night.

That the Germans had made a determined attack was shown by the statement in the communique issued later, that our night intruders had destroyed twelve enemy aircraft.

During the morning of D Plus One (Wednesday, June 7th) the British flotilla leader *Faulkner* steamed into the anchorage. There was nothing remarkable about the arrival of another warship, but many eyes were on the trim destroyer. Word had gone round that she was bringing the Commander-in-Chief of the Allied land forces, General Montgomery. As the ship came in it was possible to see the famous figure in the double-badged beret standing on the bridge.

Soon after his arrival General Montgomery paid a visit to the headquarters ship. As he came aboard, squadrons of Marauders roared overhead. About eighty machines glittered in the sunlight as they slipped over the French coast. Montgomery did not look up. He moved quickly across the deck and up an iron gangway in the company of the senior officers who had met him. After a brief conference he was ready to leave.

Recalling his last-minute broadcast in which he had wished all his troops " good hunting," I ventured to ask the General, who I first had the pleasure of meeting in France at the beginning of the war, " How is the hunting going, sir ? "

Pausing only for a moment, his face relaxed into a slight smile, and he said, " Very well—everything is going excellently." Then he was on his way again. The boat taking him back to France threaded its way through a mass of shipping and the guns of the *Belfast*, engaged in bombarding a target well out of sight from the sea, thundered as though they were sounding a salute for the General.

Words that he had used after Dunkirk came back to me : " Make it quite clear that whatever else happened, the British Army stood no nonsense from the Germans." There was a look about " Monty " which suggested that the whole of the Allied armies were going to stand even less nonsense this time.

The improvement in the weather had helped considerably, and the general situation on D Plus One was considered satisfactory. It was admitted on the naval side that the bad weather conditions had been an initial handicap, but after thirty-six hours they were able to say that all their commitments to the assault force were completely satisfied.

Speaking of the first twenty-four hours, an officer said, " We were behind because the weather was all against us. We have had to suffer far more from the weather than from the enemy, but everything has got here, including the minor landing craft."

An interesting arrival was the first of the old freighters which were later sunk end to end to provide an artificial shelter near the shore for the small boats. These shelters, which were very valuable whenever the wind got up, were called " Gooseberries " and are not to be confused with the much more ambitious floating ports which were constructed in huge sections towed from England and which were known as " Mulberries."

There was official confirmation that nothing had been

seen of German naval forces. A Norwegian destroyer, which had been lost, was believed to be the victim of a mine.

Enemy air activity remained spasmodic, and in the only conflict which might be termed a battle six F.W. 190's had been shot down. An L.C.T. had made the polite signal : " I beg to report that I shot down one Dornier aircraft last night."

On land the situation was satisfactory, although the enemy were making desperate attempts to hold up our advance in the direction of Caen. Reports coming back spoke of the magnificent work of the British paratroops. German opposition in their areas had been crushed so rapidly that important military objectives, such as bridges, locks and canal installations, had fallen intact into their hands.

Of twelve hundred aircraft engaged in our airborne landings only thirty-seven were lost in the initial stages, I heard.

Having helped to convey the Canadians to France, we felt a special interest in their doings. We were delighted, therefore, to hear that the 3rd Canadian Division had reached Carpiquet and were already eight miles inland. Equally cheering was the news that forward elements of the British 50th Division were entering Bayeux and not meeting much opposition.

These successes spurred on the men still labouring on and off the beaches. It was realised that, whatever the weather conditions, supplies must get in over the beaches to keep our troops going.

News was scarce from the American assault areas, but we understood that the U.S. troops were in, although they had met with fierce resistance on some of their beaches.

We began to hear great accounts of the Royal Marine Commando which had made the crossing in our company. It was their task to capture Port en Besin, a small but important harbour in the gap between the British and American beach-heads. The main defences of the port were three strong points chiefly designed to meet attack from the sea.

The Marines, deciding that on this occasion it would

be better to fight as soldiers rather than sailors, chose to go for their objective from the land. They had to advance ten miles through enemy held territory before they could make their attack. Their landing was planned to take place at Le Hamel, but as their vessels closed the shore they came under heavy fire from a German battery at Longues. The Marines were forced to move a mile to the eastward and then their landing was sufficiently disastrous to dishearten most troops. Five of their fourteen L.C.A.'s were mined and sunk. Many of the Marines had to swim ashore with what equipment they could salvage.

They started their march inland, and fully re-armed themselves with weapons captured from the enemy. In anticipation of such circumstances they had received training in the use of such enemy weapons as the M.G. 34, the German light machine-gun. Moving in through Les Roquettes and St. Come-de-fresne to La Rosiere, the Commando men ran into heavy German mortar fire. It was necessary to quell several machine-gun posts, and the British troops were surprised to find that Russians and Poles, forced to serve in the German Army, were among the crews they overcame.

The Marines were heavily loaded with mortar ammunition and equipment. It has been estimated that every man carried a load of nearly three-quarters of a hundredweight. Nevertheless, it was decided that they must cut across country to avoid the delay that repeated actions with machine-gun posts along the road were causing them.

When the Commando men reached their objective for the night—Hill 72, immediately south of Port en Besin—more captured arms were distributed. Their preparations to carry out the assault were aided first by the Navy, then by the R.A.F., and finally by the Army. The port was heavily bombarded by units of the Royal Navy. Then R.A.F. bombers and rocket-firing fighters came in and finally gunners on the beach put down a heavy screen of smoke shells.

96

Through the smoke the Marines went in and, after
stiff fighting, overcame the three strongpoints. German
flak-ships in the harbour joined in the fight, but the
Marines silenced them with machine-gun and mortar fire.

The hardest fighting of all was for the third and most
powerful strongpoint. The Germans twice counter-
attacked and won back the point after the Marines had
first taken it. Only when they took it for the third
time were the British left in undisputed possession.

While the fight for this last strongpoint was in progress
the Germans launched a strong counter-attack on the
Royals' base on Hill 72. Following a heavy mortar
bombardment, the enemy overran the position, causing
the small British forces to scatter. The Commando men
joined up with the force attacking the strongpoint and
helped in the final taking of it.

When they moved again to retake Hill 72 they found that
the Germans had had enough—they had withdrawn. The
Marines made contact with the Americans to the west and
linked the whole Allied front until the Army took over.

One of the Commando men to engage in this grim
battle got back to England, although his leg had been
amputated. He was Marine George Hargrave, of Glasgow, who was taken prisoner by the Germans when a
rearguard was overwhelmed by heavy mortar and
machine-gun fire.

After being taken prisoner, Hargrave was moved to a
village inland. Here is his own story, told later, of
what happened then : " I was just having a cigarette
when our Typhoons came over and flattened the village
with their bombs. Then they opened up with cannon
fire, and I was hit in the leg. For the rest of the day I
lay in a field watching our own aircraft attacking the
villages in which the Germans were trying to conceal
themselves. I had no medical attention, but one of
our fellows who was also a prisoner put a field dressing
on my leg. At night the Germans took me in a truck
to a field hospital. My leg was amputated and I was a
bit dazed and do not quite remember whether it was

the next day or the day after that the Germans moved again and I was put into another truck. After going a few miles, we halted and I was taken out and put on the roadside with two other British walking wounded. Suddenly the Germans packed up and drove off, leaving us behind. After a bit one of my pals decided to have a look round, and found a Frenchman working in a field. He got help and I was carried to his farm, where we were all looked after very well. That night he got into touch with the Americans, and they came and moved us."

The Rev. Derrick Lovell Williams, Chaplain to the Forces, Royal Marine Commando, who was killed on D Day, was at Stepney during the early blitzing of London. His former vicar subsequently described him as " fearless " and " the sort of boy who was always in the middle of it and would get the V.C. or be killed."

At home on D Plus One Mr. A. V. Alexander, First Lord of the Admiralty, sent this message to shipyard workers and those engaged in docks and on the repair of landing craft :

" I send you this message upon a historic occasion. Four long years of endurance and hardship came yesterday to their eagerly-awaited climax. . Yesterday was for all of you in the shipyards and allied industry throughout the country a day of reward. But it brings upon you a new stage in the war for which energy and determination must be doubled."

" The country waits upon the outcome of these first weeks of struggle. The enemy knows that the Allies, with your industry in the van, have built up mighty forces which can send his armies reeling backward. The enemy will endeavour to sap the strength of the Allies before their full might is upon him. Fear inspires that policy and fear makes it formidable. You and the Navy working as one can frustrate him."

" I am certain that once more you will play your part by keeping the ships of the Royal Navy fighting fit and by maintaining the great flow of shipping which will supply to all the services the tools to finish the job."

VI

INTO FRANCE

They never go to battle, but other in the defence of their own country, or to drive out of their friends' land the enemies that be comen in, or by their power to deliver from the yoke and bondage of tyranny some people that be oppressed with tyranny.

SIR THOMAS MORE.

VI

INTO FRANCE

The Navy has a way of establishing a routine in double-quick time. In war, as in peace, much of the daily life of a ship's company follows a set routine, but, in addition to that, new problems are met by new " drills." It was not surprising, therefore, that before the nightfall on D Plus One there was a good deal that was routine about life in the *Hilary* and about the way things were going on generally in the anchorage.

Naval routine does not always meet with unqualified approval inside the service. In peace-time, when ships are manned by long-service officers and men and perhaps a few members of the R.N.R. and R.N.V.R., there are not many complaints, but in war-time, when the great majority of officers and men are civilians-turned-sailors, there is frequently a mild perplexity, if not complaint.

It became a routine in the anchorage to " make smoke " each evening. This meant that strong smoke floats were set off fore and aft in the ships, and in a very short time a swirling fog enveloped the whole of the area. I was told that the effect from the air of such a screen is startling. " Ships disappear just as completely as if they had sunk beneath the waves," an Air Force officer said.

Another effect is that experienced in the ships themselves. There are very few vessels to-day that do not have an automatic air-pumping system to supply the interior compartments. When smoke is being made these suction pumps pick up their quota of artificial fog and spread it around below decks.

Each evening in the big ward-room of the *Hilary* somebody would start to cough and then people on the other side of the room would become slightly blurred and there would be the muttered explanation, " Making smoke again."

The only thing that led to any questioning of this routine was that we made smoke almost invariably before any alert was sounded, choked for half an hour or so and had emerged into " the clear " again by the time enemy planes arrived in the vicinity.

There could never be any question as to when we were making smoke, but if anybody could have overlooked the fact, the appearance of " Chiefy " would have been a reminder. Normally a man of abstemious habits, he invariably came in with his nose wrinkled in disgust when smoke was about and ordered a " night-cap " to clear his throat.

It was his proud boast that the Germans had not kept him out of his bunk on one single night during the war, and he saw no reason to miss turning in just because we were off the Normandy beaches. He was often up until one or two in the morning working out his menus for the following day, arranging the issue of supplies and seeing that hot cocoa was available for those on watch, but I do not think he missed turning in on a single night between D Day and D plus Twelve, when I made my departure from the *Hilary*.

He hardly permitted his mind to be taken off the subject of the feeding arrangements of the ship for a moment. At work in his cabin when the rattle of anti-aircraft fire outside was like a thousand stones being shaken in a giant tin box, he would say without lifting his head, " Noisy lot of devils ! "

One disturbed night we talked about his department, and I still have the carefully-written figures set down by " Chiefy," who, absorbed in his subject, was oblivious to the noise outside. He gave me the quantities of various foodstuffs required by the *Hilary*. They provided a startling indication of the enormous totals needed for the four thousand vessels in the invasion fleets.

These were the figures for the *Hilary*:

Amount of flour on board	-		32,000 lbs.
Bread required per day	-	-	750 lbs. (186 loaves)
Potatoes on board	-	-	12 tons.
Potatoes used per day	-	-	8 cwts.
Meat on board -	-	-	- 50,000 lbs.
Meat used per day	-	-	750 lbs.
Sugar on board	-	-	10,000 lbs.
Sugar used per day -		-	140 lbs.
Tea on board -	-	-	2,000 lbs.
Tea used per day	-	-	24 lbs.
Tins of milk on board	-	-	7,800
Jam and marmalade on board -			5,000 lbs.

The list was anything but complete, as the Chief went on to show by producing a copy of the General Mess Menu. It covered the whole week, and here are the menus for two typical days :

Breakfast : Oatmeal porridge, calves' liver cutlets and brown gravy.
Dinner : Vegetable soup, roast beef, roast potatoes, mashed swede and turnips, semolina milk pudding.
Tea : Bread and jam.
Supper : Lancashire hot-pot, haricot beans.

SECOND DAY :
Breakfast : Oatmeal porridge, fried egg and bacon.
Dinner : Tomato soup, roast pork, roast potatoes and cabbage, plums and custard.
Tea : Bath buns.
Supper : Fried fish and chipped potatoes.

This particular conversation ended, I remember, by " Chiefy " saying, " Live well, don't they ? " and when I agreed, adding with a deep chuckle, " And so they damn well deserve to ! "

The needs of the *Hilary* in the way of food supplies could be taken as a fair average. Some of the invasion ships would have needed much more, while the requirements of others would be considerably less.

Extensive storage space is needed for these quantities of foodstuffs. It was estimated, for instance, that eight merchant ships, which arrived off the beaches about this

time, had store space between them such as would have
housed sufficient food for a town of 40,000 inhabitants
for two months.

Fine white bread was served to the invasion forces,
but this was not a luxury. White flour had been issued
to the ships because the bread made from it keeps
better than bread made from other types of flour.

Far away on the right of our anchorage we could see
the flash of naval guns supporting the Americans on
Omaha and other beach areas. Information was getting
through in dribs and drabs, but we did know that, on
one sector, the Americans had had to face what was
probably the toughest resistance to the actual assault
on the beaches.

The story of a United States destroyer sunk on D Day
reached me later. Transports were being led in by this
and other destroyers when a German shore battery opened
up. The enemy guns were silenced by the warships but
then another battery, situated behind some hills, carried
on the firing. One of the U.S. destroyers had got off
four hundred rounds at the battery when she herself was
hit. She lost all electric power and began to go in a
circle. Using manual apparatus, the crew managed to
get the ship on a straight course again, but then her
engine-rooms flooded and she stopped dead.

The duel with the shore batteries was at its height and
the other destroyers were racing up and down, firing at
the German guns. Attempts were made to get the
damaged ship ready for towing, but before she could be
taken in tow it was obvious that she was sinking fast.
The order to abandon ship was given, and by the time
the commanding officer went over the side, the main
decks of the destroyer were already under water.

As the crew struggled in the sea, shells from the enemy
shore guns fell among them. There were many curious
currents in the sea, and one officer found after swimming
steadily for an hour he had not covered more than a
hundred yards from where the ship sank. After nearly
two hours, another destroyer got in among the survivors

with nets and boats lowered on one side while her guns still engaged the enemy on the other.

Two hours after that, with the commanding officer of the sunken destroyer on the bridge of the ship that had rescued him, the troops were able to pour ashore from the transports, the German guns having been silenced.

In the *Hilary*, a British ship, we were naturally keen to know what was happening to our own troops ; we also had a " domestic " interest in the Canadians, and, in addition, I found a wide concern as to how the Americans were getting on.

Admiral Ramsay had told us : " It is not really a case of Allied navies in this operation—it is one great navy." Still, it was a wonderful thought that a very large proportion of the Western task force was flying the Stars and Stripes. We hoped the luck would be with these brothers-in-arms who had come so far to fight with us in these memorable battles.

On the radio we heard of the American reaction to the news of invasion—of President Roosevelt leading the nation in prayer, of churches open day and night, of fifty thousand persons gathering in Madison Square Park, New York, and of the Statue of Liberty floodlit for the first time since the attack on Pearl Harbour.

There were also quoted the comments of famous newspapers, such as the *New York Times*, which recalled Hitler's boast after Dieppe that the Allies would be fortunate if they stayed for nine hours the next time they attempted to invade Europe.

" Hitler's illusion disappeared in the smoke and thunder of the Allied assault which crashed through with far less cost or difficulty than had been anticipated," said this newspaper. " To-day the Allies stand on firm land in France. They have established their beachheads ; they have cleared them of the enemy ; they have connected some of them. They control the sea-lanes and the supply routes, they control the skies. They have passed successfully, and even brilliantly, through the first critical stage. . . ."

America, too, had faith in our arms, and we felt the whole weight of a mighty nation behind our shoulders.

In the anchorage we also had the feeling that we had passed successfully through the " first critical stage." But we were still in the front line of the battle and we waited for the enemy to counter attack.

By the evening of D plus One the weather had vastly improved. The sea was comparatively smooth and " ducks " were beginning to swarm around the supply ships.

Notes that I made at the time remind me that the battleship *Rodney* was firing with her main armaments from a point fifteen miles away across the bay to the east. Every time the sixteen-inch shells were sent hurtling towards the German guns around Le Havre, the whole side of the battleship was enveloped momentarily in a sheet of flame. After an appreciable lapse of time, there followed the deep rumble of the guns.

A signal made by the *Rodney* about this time caused amusement. "Fired upon by enemy battery," she reported. "Silenced battery with two rounds of six-inch," she added, rather suggesting that her main armament was reserved for something more important than indiscreet German coastal batteries.

As night fell, a curious calm came over the shipping in the anchorage. The Germans had had time to muster their air forces and we suspected that it might be the calm before the storm.

In a sense it was, although the air attack that went on almost continuously throughout the night produced a volume of noise and disturbance that was quite out of proportion to the very limited amount of damage done on the beaches or off-shore. Most of the noise was made by our own defences. The first enemy aircraft appeared over the beaches seven or eight miles away to the west. One followed their course by a hundred curving lines of tracer. The shells made strange patterns in the sky, weaving and twisting as if giant fingers were gathering up the threads from above.

It was an absorbing sight—until the guns in the *Hilary* and a dozen other ships in the immediate vicinity took up the bombardment. Their urgent rat-rat-rat-rat shook one into a sense of danger which led to a sudden dive for cover.

The novelty of the firework display soon wore off but, unhappily, there was no escape from it. "Escape," indeed, was the word, because it soon became apparent that some of the ships in the wide anchorage were in as much danger from our own falling shells as from the German bombs. It was possible to follow the course of shells, fired on a low trajectory, which dropped into the sea not far from our own ships. In the words of one of our own gunners, it was "a proper free for all!" How the enemy planes came out of it I cannot say, because there were times when the whole sky was alight with soaring tracer.

During one particularly intense period, heavier guns joined in and, instinctively, Standing, McNichol and I got down on all fours. McNichol disappeared round a corner of the bridge and Standing made to follow. I, bringing up the rear, found myself mixed up with McNichol's head and arms and Standing's remarkably long legs. The Australian had decided that there was even less protection in the direction he was going and, returning, had collided head-on with the well-known broadcaster. It was no time for apologies and we settled down in a heap on the deck.

It was only in subsequent nights that we learned that the nightly visitations were more noisy than dangerous.

Next morning, Thursday, D plus Two, I set foot in France. The point of entry for me was the little town of Bernieres, which the Canadians had stormed into at just about the same hour two days earlier.

Going slowly towards the beaches in a duck, one understood how exposed the assault troops felt as they approached the shore when it was still in the hands of the enemy. A group of smashed-up landing craft away to the left was sufficient evidence that shells and bullets had whistled across the beaches, despite the massive bombardment. The little bunch of torn and battered craft, I learned, were the victims of one German gun right on the edge of the sea, which survived the close-in shelling from the ships. It only lasted for a few minutes after the Canadians landed, but in that time fifty of the assault troops had been made casualties.

Of that very section of wide, sandy beach Commander MacRitchie wrote : " The flotilla leader's lamp flashed and in a second we were line abreast and striking for the beach of Bernieres-sur-mer at full speed. Those soldier boys from Galt and Kitchener and Cape Breton and Toronto and Brantford and a hundred villages and hamlets have courted death a hundred times since we set them down that morning, but I doubt very much if the thrill of that drive through the sea to Bernieres will ever leave them. We who had lived in cramped quarters in the ship with them for days and had eaten out of the same ration tins, cried to them as they stood nearly two hundred strong in our ship with their packs and their bicycles and their rifles ready to land. We cried to them : ' Hold tight, we are going in.' They held tight, and in almost a split second we had crashed our way head on, right on to the sand, right over the mines and booby traps. The Nazi death-dealing appliances were exploding all around us, but these men of the Third Division never faltered. The ramps went crashing to the beach ; the soldiers grabbed their gear and, after wading ashore up to their armpits, with rifles and bicycles held high, were piped up the beaches by their regimental pipers. . . ."

And two mornings later, many of the obstacles were still present on the beach. Many were high and dry, but others were just ugly iron shapes rising out of the water. Immediately beyond the beach there were some shallow sandy dunes and a wide trench fringed with barbed wire. Beyond were a few houses and a narrow, dusty lane leading from the beach to the little town a few hundred yards inland.

The sappers had torn a wide gap in the beach obstacles, and ducks, keeping to a narrow mine-free track, were passing through. They shook themselves free of water and, with a grunt of changing gears, lumbered up the sands as wheeled vehicles.

They arrived on the road under the eye of the Naval Beachmaster, a bearded Commander armed with a megaphone which he seldom needed. " Keep moving ! " was the cry as loading papers were snatched as the ducks went by. A metal network had been put down to bind the sand into a firm surface, and the ducks kept moving. Farther along the beach similar vehicles were coming back from unloading their stores and going out to sea for more. The first supply-belt for the invasion armies had already been established.

Climbing on to the dunes, I looked back across the anchorage and up and down the beaches. There was life and movement everywhere. Ships and landing craft were coming and going, amphibious vehicles formed a direct contact between sea and land, and soldiers on shore were busy handling stores and improving their anti-aircraft gun sites.

In this one section of beach alone, dozens of landing craft were high and dry on the sand, with their " mouths " wide open to permit of the rapid landing of the sinews of war. The Navy was all out to catch up the unloading schedule, put behind time by the unexpectedly bad weather conditions of the previous two days.

The fields behind the dunes were still empty, although the army could have made good use of this additional space. German " Minen " signs, with a grim outline of a skull and cross-bones on them, explained why these fields could not be used.

" Keep clear of the verges " was one of the first warnings I heard. Numerous vehicles had finished their invasion days on one of the mines left along the roadside by the Germans. To clear the verges so that it was safe for our big tanks and transports to pull a yard or two off the highway was the immediate task of the sappers.

Later, with special flail tanks, they would clear the fields.

Turning towards the road I met some excited soldiers who told me that " Monty " had just driven through the village in a duck. " Thought it wouldn't be long before he came ashore," they said. " He's a proper——!" They swore in full-blooded appreciation. As far as I went along that road on D plus Two, I heard the same thing. The troops talked of the snipers still at work along the roads and there was a note of anxiety about their leader.

I, too, was warned about these snipers. " Had two of our fellows wounded on this corner early this morning," a corporal said. He looked suspiciously at a few French villagers and there were open suggestions that nobody was to be trusted.

A Canadian sentry at the entrance to the drive of a large house told me that shooting had been going on all night, although all organised forms of resistance had been broken more than twenty-four hours earlier. He indicated a still figure, covered with a blanket, lying just inside the gates. " That is what happened to one of our own fellows who forgot the password," he said.

That German snipers were about, possibly dressed in civilian clothes or even masquerading as women, I could believe. That the French were taking any part in the shooting I could not believe.

A military policeman on traffic duty was telling me that bullets had whistled near him on several occasions, when a French boy dashed up on a bicycle. " Where have they taken my brother ? " he asked.

I passed the question on, and then explained to the boy in my limited French that his brother had been taken to the beaches and would probably be sent to England. The French lad thanked me and set off again on his bicycle. Later in the morning I saw him arrive with his mother at a British army post on the beaches. His brother was being held under armed escort.

Apparently the youth under arrest had rushed into his home, shouting the names of some Germans and saying, " They are here ! " But the Germans had already gone and the Canadians were in the house. They promptly arrested the lad, and the question that had to be cleared up was whether he had intended to help the enemy by giving them warning.

These are the facts of the case as they were given to me and I have no knowledge of how the matter ended.

I had not reached the centre of Bernieres, however, before I had an encounter which I much prefer to think gave the true reflection of the people of Normandy to the invasion. An elderly man came riding towards me on a bicycle which appeared to be too big for him. It wobbled as he raised his head to look in my direction. "*Bon jour, m'sieur,*" I said, and the old gentleman surprised me by jumping off the bicycle like a youngster and almost running across the road to greet me in return. Could I speak French ? he wanted to know, and if I could, would I talk to him ?

There have been many events since which leave no doubt as to where the French stood. The valiant part they played in freeing their own country of the hated Boche was proof of their staunchness in adversity. But my contact with the old Frenchman was a very early one and his reactions to the Allied invasion are therefore worthy of record.

The menace of the Germans was still with him because, before we talked, he drew me to the side of the road, where we were partly in the shelter of a damaged house.

Then he began to speak, slowly at first, but more rapidly as his feelings carried him along.

" For four years I have been unable to say a word," he told me, putting his finger in front of his mouth in a sign of silence. "We dare not speak, although we could think all the time. I was a soldier in the last war and fought at Verdun against these very Germans. We thought we had saved France."

He paused to fumble with old hands in his loose jacket. From a pocket book he produced a faded certificate which gave the record of his service in the French army.

Then he showed me another document which revealed his age as sixty-three—he looked much older.

I asked about a tiny piece of ribbon in his button-hole. It was, as I had thought, the ribbon of the Croix de Guerre. " I have worn it all the time," he said. " I am old and it did not matter to the Germans, but still I won it fighting against them."

He straightened himself and went on : " The night before last I had gone to bed when the air-raid warnings went. I got up and went to the cellar to take shelter. It must have been about 4 a.m. when the bombs began to fall. There were big explosions and we wondered if the house would fall on us. It lasted for an hour and then something different began to happen. At first I could not believe my ears, but after a time I was sure I was right. It was attack by artillery. I recognised the sound which, as any soldier knows, is quite different to bombing. I was so excited that I climbed to the top of the house, although there were many shells. From the window I could see the bay, and there was the great English fleet. I knew the hour of liberation was at hand. I did not care then. I ran downstairs and out into the street. Others were there, and I told them what I had seen."

The Frenchman had to pause for a moment and there were tears running down his cheeks as he continued : " There was shooting in the streets and then the Tommies came along. They came down this very street, driving the Huns before them. We saw it all and there were Canadians with them who saw us and shouted to us in French. I ran to the beach, where there was still fighting. But it was magnificent—the great fleet in the bay. I stood, I cannot say how long, watching the wonderful organisation of the disembarkation."

These were deeply-moving words, spoken with a fierce sincerity, and I patted the Frenchman on the shoulder. He was crying openly as he leaned forward and kissed me lightly on both cheeks. Then he took a step back and saluted. We shook hands and I went on up the

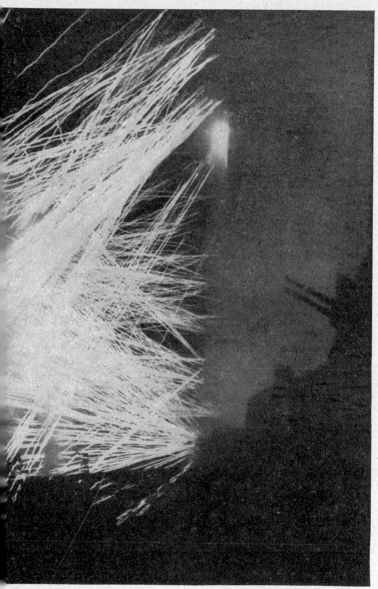

NIGHT TRACER PATTERN FROM THE GUNS OF THE INVASION FLEET REPULSING ENEMY RAIDERS

(Crown copyright reserved)

16-IN. AND 6-IN. GUNS OF THE BRITISH BATTLESHIP "RODNEY" POUND THE ENEMY OVER THE NORMANDY BEACHES

(Crown copyright reserved)

road. I think the little Frenchman knew that I could not have spoken to him at that moment, anyway.

As I walked along the road between houses which had all been damaged in the bombardment, I noticed that the Croix de Lorraine had already been chalked on many of them. That this symbol of freedom had been put there by the French people was proved to me in a curious way. A Frenchwoman approached me anxious for information. There was little I could tell her, but she was grateful. From her finger she took a ring and asked me to inspect the inside of it. There, neatly engraved, I saw the sign which, if the Germans had discovered it, would certainly have cost her her freedom.

A few French flags had begun to appear in Bernieres, and there was one big Canadian flag which must have gone in with the assault troops. " V " signs were also to be seen, and the British troops, moving up in lorries, had roses in their steel helmets.

In the main square of Bernieres there were still many signs of the fighting that had gone on there only a few hours earlier. A shell had drilled a large hole through the steeple of the big church, where snipers had been located after the Germans had been pushed out of the town. On a stone column in front of the church were the words : " Mort Pour la France, 1914–18."

A map had been sketched on a blackboard and the line of the British and Canadian advance was roughly drawn upon it. The French people, gathered around the board, discussed the situation animatedly.

They spoke of General de Gaulle's call to them : " The supreme battle is engaged. After so many struggles, so much fury, so much pain, we are now faced with the decisive blow, the blow for which we have hoped so much. It is, it should be understood, the Battle of France, and it is the battle waged by France. . . . For the sons of France, wherever they may be, or whoever they may be, the simple and sacred duty is to fight by every means at their disposal."

They repeated the words of General Eisenhower's

Proclamation : " Le jour de la délivrance se lève. Vos frères d'armes sont maintenant sur le sol français . . . . Nous arrivons tous unis pour mettre fin sur le champ de bataille à la guerre que vous avez menée si héroïquement à travers les années de farouche résistance. Nous détruirons la tyrannie nazie dans ses racines et ses rameaux, afin que les peuples d'Europe renaissent dans la liberté."

A sign-post in Bernieres—the first blue and white French road sign I had seen for four years—said, " Caen, 20 kilometres." One thought of the hard fighting going on in those twenty kilometres and of the help that could still be given to the British and Canadian troops by the guns of the warships in the bay.

I wondered if they would hear the good news contained in the official S.H.A.E.F. communique, which, after announcing the fall of Bayeux, stated : " Contact has been established between our seaborne and airborne troops. The steady build-up of our forces has continued. During the night forces of E-boats made unsuccessful attempts to interfere with the continual arrival of supplies. Support fire from Allied warships continued throughout yesterday."

There was also cheering news from the American sectors, where Rear-Admiral Hall, U.S. Navy, had paid tribute to the fine work of the United States Rangers in scaling the cliffs to put out of action important gun positions. The ships, he said, had had less trouble from mines than he had anticipated.

From England there came the careful summing-up of the Allied naval Commander-in-Chief : " Our plan was a set-piece of such momentum," said Admiral Ramsay, " that we had no doubt we should reach the other side. But there was some doubt about the losses. We have got one hundred per cent. of the assault across. We are not going in just to hold a bridgehead, but to make a bridge into France."

VII

THE BAY OF THE SEINE

The Royal Navy of England hath ever been its greatest defence and ornament ; it is its ancient and natural strength.

SIR WILLIAM BLACKSTONE.

VII

THE BAY OF THE SEINE

THE bombardment of enemy positions and concentrations inland by Allied battleships and cruisers continued unabated. Among the British ships H.M.S. *Ramillies*, built twenty-eight years earlier on the Clyde, was well to the fore.

Two gun crews, one a naval crew commanded by Lieut. Robert Dunn, R.N., of Portsmouth, and the other a Royal Marine crew commanded by Lieut. R. Miles, R.M., of Hove, fired alternately from different 15-inch turrets from D Day to D plus Ten. In that time nearly a thousand tons of shells were directed on to enemy targets from the old British battleship.

Watching the *Ramillies* in action, I recalled the days spent in her before the war when two hundred young seamen were receiving their early training in the ship. Coming south from Lamlash, there were exercises in the Irish Channel and further out in the Atlantic. I speculated as to whether any of the keen youngsters I had watched were serving in the ship for the bombardment.

I knew that the gun crews, working so smoothly in the turrets, would see little of what was going on outside, although modern loud-speaker equipment enables a running commentary on the shoot to be broadcast inside the turret.

But the men in the shell-room and magazine are cut off even from this. In the *Ramillies* they were working deep down in the ship for hours on end. They handled over a thousand tons of shells and thousands of pounds of cordite.

At one point in the bombardment the *Ramillies* lost contact with the aircraft which was giving her aerial direction. A good deal of amusement was caused by a sergeant pilot in another aircraft which took over the

" spotting." He first apologised over the radio for any short-comings, explaining that " he had never done that sort of thing before."

He said he would do his best, although he did not know the correct phraseology for directing the fire. For a short time a startled gunnery control in the battleship received a series of unorthodox messages such as " Damned near, but a bit short," " Try to pitch them a bit higher," " A bit more to the right, and you've got them," " That's the stuff," " You have hit the railway ! "

After ten days Sergeant H. F. Simmonds, Royal Marines, of Brighton, who was captain of " X " turret, said, " Although it was the biggest shoot I have experienced in ten years' service, the whole series of engagements went off so smoothly that it was like some giant exercise. After the first few rounds there was nothing in it." Among congratulatory signals on the accuracy of the fire from the *Ramillies* was one from the *Nelson*, a ship with even larger turrets.

Among the ships that took part in the great bombardment which harried the Germans until they had retreated inland out of range of even the most powerful naval guns were the British battleships *Nelson*, *Rodney* and *Warspite*, the U.S. battleships *Texas*, *Nevada* and *Arkansas* (the first two " ghosts " from the " graveyard " of Pearl Harbour), the British cruisers *Apollo*, *Argonaut*, *Belfast*, *Bellona*, *Black Prince*, *Ceres*, *Danae*, *Arethusa*, *Diadem*, *Enterprise*, *Frobisher*, *Glasgow*, *Hawkins*, *Mauritius*, *Orion* and *Scylla*, the U.S. cruisers *Tuscaloosa*, *Augusta* and *Quincy*, the British monitor *Roberts* and the Polish cruiser *Dragon*.

Credit has been given to the *Rodney* and *Ramillies* for breaking up a German counter-attack north-west of Caen by which the enemy hoped to split the British and American armies.

The big naval guns also played a vital part in protecting the exposed flank of the Allied forces in the direction of Le Havre.

The bombardment by the big ships, however, was

only one angle of the operations. In the words of the First Lord of the Admiralty about this time, " The Navy's job is only just beginning. It has to continue pouring men across the Channel into France until the enemy is beaten. There is an unlimited demand—a blank cheque—on the sea power of the United Nations."

This was emphasised by Admiral Harold R. Stark, Commander, U.S. Naval Forces in Europe, when he said in a broadcast to America, " An Allied overseas operation of a magnitude unparalleled in history is now taking place. The United States Navy have worthily played their part. It is a moment for paying homage to the men who have long prepared for and who are now so valiantly carrying out their tasks. I wish I could mention every man jack in this operation, whether navy, or coast-guard, or merchant marine, not only the highest ranking officers, but all hands. Team-work, high spirit, courage are traditional in our maritime services. Those qualities are abundantly evident in these narrow seas to-day. In this team hundreds of thousands of families in our country are represented. You have reason to be proud of your men. All are performing magnificently, whether in the air, in the battleships, in the smallest craft, or on the beaches. The toughness of the days immediately ahead and of the days beyond must not be minimised. Our combined navies and merchant navies are providing a bridge from these islands to France—a bridge from a free world to a world of bondage."

We had not long to wait for further evidence that the Germans were doing their best to knock a span out of that bridge.

The night of D plus 2 had been a particularly noisy one in the anchorage. Soon after dark one ship was set on fire and was soon blazing from stem to stern. There were numerous air-raid alarms and a minor battle developed between our sea patrols and German light forces.

When daylight came on D plus 3 (Friday, June 9th), the sky was overcast and conditions were all against the close air cover that had been provided up to that time.

Still the major enemy air attack which we had half expected even when the weather was better did not develop.

In a party of survivors coming to the *Hilary* was the commanding officer of a landing craft which had been blown up as it went astern off the beaches. He had a grim story to tell. While they were on the beach they had come under the fire of a German sniper. The Number One of the craft was wounded in the chest. The young skipper knew that it was serious and made a signal to another ship which came near to him, " Have man who is dying—expert attention may save his life." The other vessel had to answer, " Sorry, have sixty like that here."

Some of those who had died on the beaches, I heard, were washed back on the following high tide. " They appeared to be on their hands and knees, face down to the water," an officer said.

Generally the news remained good. The supply ships were getting in and the British anchorage—thirty miles long and seven miles deep—was as full as we had seen it. The artificial inshore protection for small craft, known as the Gooseberry, was well under way. The old tramp-ships that were to be sunk end to end to make this " harbour " came in under their own steam. Old and rusted as they were, it was a sad sight if one did not remember that they, who had served their country so well, were still going to be of service after they had settled on to the bed of the sea. The *Empire Bunting*, the *Bendoran*, the *Empire Moorhen*, the *Empire Waterhen*, the *Mariposa* and the rest, they came in without fuss and headed inshore close to where they were to be sunk.

The first of them, we heard, had already settled down on the sandy bottom with big, gaping holes in their sides. The tide would rise and fall inside them, but, at high or low tide, they would continue to protect the hundreds of little vessels from the buffeting of the open sea.

There was also news that the first R.A.F. group headquarters had gone ashore and that two emergency landing grounds and one renewal and re-armament strip were in operation. On the beaches and beyond, searchlights had been put in position to help our A.A. gunners.

On this day, too, the first hospital ship steamed into the British anchorage. What might have been the cause of much additional suffering to our wounded was largely discounted by the fact that a number of the commodious L.S.T.'s had been especially fitted out to take wounded men. Not only had they comfortable bunks for 400, but there were also emergency operating theatres.

Some days later I watched one of these craft unloading in a British port. Only a minute or two after its arrival stretcher bearers were passing over the ramp, and the men they carried were placed in waiting ambulances which set off at once for military hospitals in the vicinity.

Among the many light craft moving among the bigger ships off the French coast were the eighty-feet cutters of the U.S. Coastguards. They had been doing excellent work, especially in saving men from drowning when ships and craft sank on their way to the beaches. They went to within a thousand yards of the beaches, and one cutter, commanded by Lieut. R. V. McPhail, of Carolina, saved 126 men from three different vessels.

Another Coastguard cutter took thirty men off a sinking L.C.T., including one wounded man who had to be lowered into the water before he could be got on board the American boat. A member of the crew of the cutter went on to the sinking L.C.T. to do this and only learned later, when the landing craft blew up, that he had been standing on tons of ammunition.

In the early hours of D plus Four (Saturday, June 10th) our naval forces guarding the western approach to the sea-lanes and the Normandy anchorage clashed with German forces attempting to break through the screen.

It was a full-scale destroyer action in which British Tribal-class ships measured themselves against German Roeder-class vessels. The result no doubt convinced the Germans that we were well prepared to deal with any attempt to attack in force with surface craft. Two enemy destroyers were sunk and two damaged. All our ships returned safely, although one was hit and set on fire for a short time.

The German destroyers, which were provided with air cover, were detected as they attempted to move up Channel under cover of batteries on the French coast. The force, which was believed to have sailed from Brest, was strong enough to have inflicted heavy damage on our shipping if it had rounded the Cherbourg peninsula. Roeder-class destroyers are over 400 feet long and have an armament of five 5·9-inch guns and two quadruple mounting torpedo tubes. Their speed is said to approach forty knots.

It was truly an Allied force that engaged the enemy, there being units of the Royal Navy, the Royal Canadian Navy and the Polish Navy. Among the ships there were H.M.S. *Tartar*, H.M.S. *Ashanti*, H.M.C.S. *Haida*, H.M.C.S. *Huron*, H.M.S. *Eskimo*, H.M.S. *Javelin* and the Polish destroyers *Blyskawicka* and *Piorun*.

The action opened at 1.25 A.M. Visibility was low when the Allied ships, led by the *Tartar*, sighted four enemy destroyers. Determined offensive action was taken at once, and the enemy promptly turned and steamed to the westward, making smoke as they went. After a hit had been scored by the *Haida* the Germans launched a strong torpedo attack and the Allied vessels were forced to take avoiding action. The leading German ship turned to the north, separating from the rest. She was at once engaged by the *Tartar* and hits were obtained. At the same time the *Ashanti* was inflicting heavy punishment on another of the enemy destroyers.

Towards the end of the first stage of the action the

Tartar was hit and set on fire. Part of the mast was shot away and the British vessel was forced to turn away in order to get the fire under control.

Seeing the *Tartar* in distress, the *Ashanti* swung round and attacked the German destroyer with torpedoes. At 2.37 A.M. there was a tremendous explosion as the enemy vessel blew up.

The *Tartar* was still steaming at slow speed when she encountered another of the Roeders which had apparently been hit earlier. The *Tartar* opened up with all her guns from a range of about 500 yards. The enemy was enveloped in smoke, but the contact was lost because the *Tartar* was in no fit state to press home the attack.

Meanwhile, the two Canadian destroyers *Haida* and *Huron* were having a battle of their own with two of the enemy destroyers. They were forced to open the range as they were running into a minefield, but one of the German ships was hit.

As they were returning to the main force, the Canadian ships made contact with another enemy destroyer on an opposite course. They immediately gave chase. Contact was lost on more than one occasion, but, speeding to the east, the Canadians managed to close the range. At 3.30 there was a heavy under-water explosion, but the German vessel continued on its course.

The enemy ship was keeping very close to the shore, but the first light of day was making it difficult for her to avoid the heavy fire of the Canadian destroyers. It was after 5 A.M. when the German destroyer was hit, despite attempts to cover her movements with smoke. She swung away to the shore in the vicinity of the Ile de Batz light and ran on to the rocks.

The other Allied ships came up and final salvoes set the German vessel on fire. As our destroyers turned to seaward there were several explosions and flames from the enemy ship rose above her mast. Steaming along the coast, the Allied force was attacked by Ju. 88's, but the enemy aircraft were driven off by gunfire.

More than a month after this action was fought I had

a curious personal contact with it. Joining a Canadian fleet minesweeper off Roscoff, I was in the wardroom when two young officers returned after a long pull in a boat. One carried a heavy ship's compass.

It was the compass of the German destroyer which had run on the rocky Brittany coast. The young Canadians had paid a visit to the victim of their own countrymen. They reported that the German vessel was lying hard on the rocks at an angle of 45 degrees. Some of the engines had been blown clean out of the ship and she was generally smashed up. The body of a German sailor was still lying by the forward gun.

At the time of the action confirmation of success came in S.H.A.E.F. Communiqué No. 9, which stated : " An enemy destroyer, driven ashore off Batz in the Brest peninsula earlier in the day by naval surface forces, was attacked and left a smouldering hulk." Other items in the same communique were : " One enemy aircraft was shot down twenty miles off Brest by anti-E-boat patrols flown over western Channel waters," and " Coastal aircraft are co-operating with naval surface forces in a vigorous offensive against U-boats which are threatening to attack our lines of communication to the assault area."

That the Navy were just as watchful well out on the eastern flank was apparent from a further communiqué on the same day, which revealed that our light coastal forces had been fighting off the Dutch coast while the destroyers were in action down the Channel. Four heavily armed trawlers had been engaged south-west of Imuiden by " little ships " under the command of Lieut.-Commander K. Gemmell, D.S.C., R.N.V.R., and three of them had been sunk by torpedoes. The other ship had been heavily damaged and had made for port. Later three other trawlers had come out, apparently searching for survivors, and one of these was also torpedoed. In the action we lost one motor-torpedo-boat, but there were only two casualties, all the rest of the crew being picked up by our own boats.

And in the anchorage, so well protected by both outer

and inner screens, there was great activity. Supplies were flowing in and there seemed to be more ducks on the delivery belt than ever before.

They were very useful if one wanted to get ashore, because, except at high tide, it was practically impossible to find a place where boats could get alongside. The beach shelves very gently and the only channel in our part of the landing area was the one leading into the tiny harbour of Courseulles.

It was a duck that came to the rescue when a boat in which I was heading for the shore, ran aground three or four hundred yards from the beach. The duck gave a fine display of its prowess in the final run to the shore. Driven by a soldier almost exactly as one would drive a car, it moved steadily through the water until its wheels touched down on the bottom. A quick movement with a lever and it was running like a truck partly submerged in water. Suddenly it lost way as we dropped into a deep pool and floated again. Immediately the duck became a boat again, driven by a screw in the stern. Then we were landborne again and the strange vehicle, once more relying on its wheel drive, slowly climbed the sands and trundled off inland.

It took me along the road from Bernieres to Courseulles. It was not a very wide road and one was not entirely oblivious to the signs still hanging on the fences either side giving warning of mines. They were German signs, displaying a skull and cross-bones on a white or yellow board. It was still the case that few of the fields were in use because the Sappers had not had time to clear them of mines.

An R.A.S.C. unit, under Major S. T. Moore, of Walton-on-Thames, which came over on D Day, had settled itself comfortably, although there had been some nocturnal searchings for German snipers. Not far from them was a field dressing station which the enemy had bombed a few hours earlier, killing four wounded Germans who were being treated at the time. British officers I talked with spoke well of a German doctor, himself a prisoner, who continued to attend to British "tommies" while German bombs fell close at hand.

Another visit I paid, after leaving the duck, was to a farm which the Germans had occupied up to the last moment. There were many signs of war but none remain more sharply in my memory than a cow which was lying in the corner of a stall. It had been wounded in the stomach during the shelling. An old Frenchman, looking at the animal with some pity, explained that most of the cattle had been killed—they were to be seen lying on their backs in the fields with their legs sticking straight up in the air—and the wounded animal would probably be good for food, if only somebody would come and buy it before it died.

The dead cows, incidentally, were put into big pits and burned, to the accompaniment of a smell which I never want to meet again.

Courseulles I found alive with troops and the M.P. controlling traffic at the cross-roads was as busy as any London traffic policeman. Entering a small courtyard, I met Lieut. Ian Higgs, R.N.V.R., of the Admiralty Press Division. A long, modern building facing us, he explained, was the former headquarters of the German army commander on this section of the coast. British shells had found the building but it was still habitable. (I gathered that a senior British naval officer had already got his eye on it).

Most interesting was a big relief plan, about the size of a large billiard table, which occupied the centre of a ground-floor room, the end of which was still dominated by a swastika painted on the wall. Every detail of the beach area was shown on the plan. There were model guns, barbed wire entanglements, strong points, sea obstructions, and vehicles. They were all connected to press-button lighting so that the model, if it had been possible to move it, would have been the most fascinating toy any boy ever had. There were even model landing craft coming in from the sea but if the German Commandant thought in terms of the half-dozen represented on the plan, he must have had the shock of his life when he looked out on the real thing.

Although the big room was in disorder, there was still a sense of military correctness about it and two huge pots of fern, which had decorated it for the Germans, still stood as lonely sentinels near the deserted swastika.

An interesting souvenir given me by Lieut. Higgs was the German Commandant's copy of " Mein Kampf." Neatly bound in a blue cover, it had a gold swastika on the front and a photo of Hitler as a frontispiece. But there was neither thumb-mark nor anything else to indicate that the book had ever been opened.

A few of the shops in Courseulles had already started business again, including the butcher and baker. The town itself did not appear to be too badly knocked about although fighting had clearly taken place in its streets. The cemetery was still closed because of the danger of mines but the Sappers were systematically clearing the ground. As they went, they turned the German warning signs round and wrote " Mines Cleared " on the other side.

Talking with some of the French people, I formed the opinion that their secret worry when the invasion started was, " Is it another big raid, like Dieppe ? Will the Germans come back ? " Their confidence had grown apace and they were really beginning to believe that they had been liberated. These, it is only fair to point out, were very early days.

Before returning to the *Hilary*, I collected one other souvenir. It was a large notice, " Choucroute garni— Chaud Samedi midi," which was given a place of honour in the ward-room anti-room.

There was little to mark our first Sunday off the Normandy beaches from any of the other days. D plus 5 (Sunday, June 11th) was just one more day in which the supplies had got to go in and every possible support be given to the men ashore. The fusion of the beach-heads had been completed and a coastal strip sixty miles long was firmly in our hands. Its depth was being steadily increased. While British and Canadian forces met heavy German pressure in the region of Caen, the Americans made further progress in the Cherbourg peninsula.

"Allied warships have been giving deep supporting fire in the centre and close support on the flanks of our armies," said Communiqué No. 14 on this day.

Not far from *Hilary* in the anchorage, H.M.S. *Belfast* and *Diadem* were providing their share of this support. One of the targets, I was told, was Carpiquet aerodrome, a mile or so to the west of Caen, which the Germans still held. The British naval guns were hitting the enemy at a range of about twelve miles. Assisted by spotters, both on land and in the air, the gunners got off a hundred rounds in very fast time.

Dozens of small craft in-shore took no notice of the bombardment although the shells, still gaining elevation, went over them on their way to the targets.

Numerous naval units had settled down in odd floating homes inside the Gooseberry and at other points off-shore. In a London barge I found Engineer officers and ratings busily at work. The barge had been given a concrete floor in the centre of which was an army-type lorry fitted with lathes and other machinery. A canvas canopy, open at both ends to admit the daylight, covered the barge. It was one of five such floating barges which had been at work in our area since D plus One. At the end of the vessel a naval blacksmith hammered away as unconcernedly as if he were close-by an English village green.

The forward part of the barge formed the crew's home. Bunks were built around the side and a suprisingly wide living space was left in the centre. The engineers had a twenty-four-hours round of duties and some of the ratings, who had worked through the night on the hundred-and-one repair jobs that had to be done for a fleet of small ships, were sleeping comfortably in their bunks.

Warrant Shipwright Cole, a Portsmouth man, declared that after twenty-four years in the Navy, including

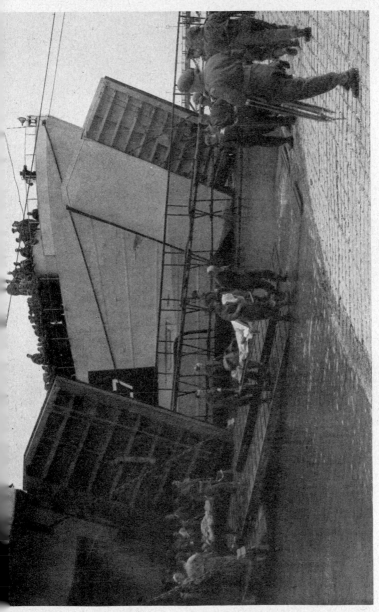

L.S.T.'S ACT AS HOSPITAL SHIPS
(Royal Canadian Navy Photograph)

service in this war in Norway, Crete and Tobruk, he was now handling the best equipment he had ever had.

Close to the workshop barge was a U.S. Navy landing craft. It was quite a small vessel but it was distinguished on account of its battle honours, painted on white squares on its side. They were : " 3rd Division, Sicily, 1943 ; British Hampshires, Salerno, 1943 ; 3rd Division, Anzio, 1944." Other white squares were ready for the Invasion honours so recently won.

Another unusual craft was the Landing Craft, Kitchen —known to the men in the anchorage as " the Coffee Stall." I went on board in time to see seven hundred dinners coming out of the ovens. The L.C.K. was designed to answer the needs of the men serving in oilers, and other small craft, where it is impossible to use a galley. By devoting one landing craft to the sole purpose of cooking, it was possible to give all these personnel hot meals.

The L.C.K. had the appearance of a houseboat which somebody had attempted to turn into a factory. Chimneys, with square cowls on them, rose up from all parts of the vessel. But when the L.C.K. made smoke nobody complained.

Ten cooks found full-time employment in her and the nine seamen in her crew spent most of their working hours as " spud bashers," as the Navy says. The roast pork, roast potatoes and peas and stewed apples and custard which I saw being placed in heat-retaining tins for despatch to the men in the small craft, looked as appetising as any food I saw while off the Invasion beaches.

At all times it was fascinating to move about in the anchorage, whether one went by open boat, or duck or fast speed boat. There were ships of all kinds playing their front line parts. On the decks of the L.S.T.'s and L.S.I.'s one saw the soldiers moving, as it were, into battle. The warships, big and small, were all ready for immediate action, the tramp steamers and the small craft moved in or out of the anchorage with purpose, knowing that they played an essential part in the whole. Even paddle steamers—London's *Golden Eagle* among them—had their place in the most complete representation of sea power I have ever seen, or will see.

And even the old sunken ships that went to make up the Gooseberry still proudly wore their Red Ensigns.

One had the same feeling, too, about the air forces. There was hardly a moment when some of our planes were not to be seen, and occasionally there were closer contacts when we heard details of individual efforts.

That night a young pilot was aboard the *Hilary*. He was an Australian, Warrant Officer Russell Thomas, from Melbourne. He was anxious to get back to England to rejoin his squadron. A few hours earlier he had flown over and gone inland with other Mustangs to " strafe " enemy supply columns. They had found and attacked about seventy German vehicles on the road. Most of the vehicles were smashed up but when Thomas turned for home he found that his plane had been hit by flak and would not " make it." He decided on a forced landing and came down in a field which was not nearly long enough for the purpose. In fact he went through the hedges of three fields before his damaged plane came to a standstill. He was just about to scramble out when he saw a party of soldiers waving to him and heard them shout that he was not to move. Then a Royal Engineer's officer approached cautiously and told him that he had landed in the middle of a minefield. Slowly the officer guided the airman to safety.

Another incident concerning a flyer which took place in the *Hilary*, had its touch of drama. One of the R.A.F. staff officers in the ship was in conversation with another young pilot who had been brought off from the shore.

The staff officer, a wireless expert, described a conversation he had had to listen to between a Squadron Leader and one of his Pilots after a sortie over the German positions. " I heard the Pilot report that his oil pressure had gone and the Squadron Leader told him that flak must have got his oil-feed, because he was throwing out a long black trail of smoke," he said. "They were flying at about 7,000 feet and the boy in the damaged plane said he would try and glide back and land inside our lines. 'Better bale out and let the crate go,' the Squadron Leader advised him, and then there was silence for a bit. Next I heard was the pilot saying that he was trying to get out but was caught up in the plane in some way. Then he said he was down to less than a thousand feet. I strained every nerve to hear and thought I heard the boy say something about 'three hundred feet,' but could not be sure. He would not have stood much chance from that height."

And then the young, fair-haired pilot shook us all by saying, with a slight smile, "No he would not, if you had heard him at three hundred feet—but thank God you did not, because I was clear of the cockpit by then."

Another R.A.F. story—this time one which everybody enjoyed—I never obtained proof of. It concerned a Flying Officer who was making a journey by road when he fell into the hands of the enemy. His captors numbered about a hundred. Sizing up the situation quickly, the officer asked if they could arrange to have him moved to a back area quickly. Asked for a reason for his request, he said, with some reluctance, that he believed powerful British forces were about to attack in that area and he did not want to be involved. Thereupon the Germans had a conference and decided to surrender to their prisoner. He set off with a hundred Huns, anxiously searching for some British troops to take the place of his imaginary force.

And the story, as the Squadron Leader who told it to me swore, ended with the Germans being safely handed over to the army !

The Fleet Air Arm itself was in the thick of it from D Day onwards. The Seafire III, the Navy's latest type of Fighter aircraft, was making its first appearance when it flew over the beaches. Squadrons of these planes were in the first wave of aircraft to take off from a naval air station in southern England before dawn on Invasion day. They carried out target reconnaissance and spotting for the warships. Aircraft of the Fighter wing at this airfield flew 435 sorties in the day—a record for any Tactical Air Force airfield in England.

Their spotting operations were completely successful and six hours after the bombardment of the shore began it was reported that every one of the original targets had either been put out of action or destroyed.

It was the first time the Navy had had an aircraft specially equipped for taking reconnaissance photographs. The Seafire III's took photographs which were of the utmost value to our Intelligence service.

A single-engined, low-winged monoplane, the Seafire III is powered with a Rolls-Royce Merlin engine which develops 1,470 horse power. It is a single-seater fighter and can operate from aircraft carriers (as it did, at a later stage, for the invasion of Southern France). Its armament is two 20 mm. cannon and four .303 Browning guns.

Another type of Navy aircraft to take part in spotting, reconnaissance and air-sea rescue work was the Sea Otter, Mark I, a single-engined amphibian biplane. In addition to three Vickers .303 " K " guns, it is fitted to carry bombs or depth charges.

Of seven naval pilots shot down on D day, four got back to England and two returned so quickly that they were on operations again the next day.

Lieut. (A) J. B. Madden, R.N.V.R. was flying over Tilly-sur-Seulles, about six miles south-east of Bayeux, when he saw a concentration of enemy tanks in the town. He reported the position to the cruiser *Orion*. When the *Orion* opened fire, she obtained a direct hit with her second shell. The Germans at once moved off to the cover of a nearby wood. Again the Seafire reported their position and the *Orion* soon had the wood under fire. The German tanks made another dash for the town and the *Orion* was hot on their trail when Lieut. Madden headed for home.

A Seafire flown by Lieut. (A) W. A. Wallace, R.N.V.R.,

was hit by flak and made a forced landing in no-man's-land. It caught fire as it hit the ground but the naval flyer scrambled out and hid in a ditch near his blazing machine. Later he was able to get back inside our positions after dodging several enemy patrols.

One of the most amazing escapes was that of Lieut. Commander P. E. I. Bailey, R.N., who led a Seafire squadron. He was flying at 12,000 feet over the beach of Le Hamel just after dawn when the tail of his aircraft was shot away. The Seafire went into a vertical spin. As the Lieut. Commander tried to climb out of the machine, the cock-pit-hood jammed and he could only get his head and shoulders free. He was only a few hundred feet from the ground when he took a desperate chance and pulled the rip-cord of his parachute, hoping that the latter would open and drag him out of the cock-pit. The chance came off and Lieut. Commander Bailey estimated subsequently that he hit the ground a couple of seconds after the parachute had arrested his fall. The Seafire crashed and exploded a hundred yards away from him. Still the naval flyer was to experience his narrowest escape from death. Before he could get free of his parachute it had dragged him across the beach and the fabric fouled a mine on a beach obstruction. The mine exploded not more than twenty yards from the Lieut. Commander. He was dazed, but otherwise suffered no injury from his series of hair-raising experiences, other than a sprained ankle ! He returned to England next day and reported for duty.

Lieut. D. B. Law, R.N.V.R., was another pilot who made a forced landing inside the enemy lines. He made a dash for our positions, got through and then insisted on returning to his machine with some heavy tools to destroy certain secret apparatus. He successfully made his escape the second time.

An R.A.F. pilot flying with a naval fighter wing, Flying Officer Duff, was shot down twice. On the second occasion, by a miracle, he succeeded in landing his machine in a field full of anti-aircraft stakes.

Lieut. Commander W. Simpson and Lieut. "Tiny" Devonald both had fights in which the odds were more than six to one against them. Devonald turned and fought eight F.W. 190's which attacked him. He had to "ditch" his own machine but was picked up and brought safely back to England.

And all these things were made possible, as the pilots themselves were only too anxious to declare, by the devotion to duty of the ratings and airmen who, as ground staff, worked twenty-four hours a day, in the early stages, and maintained ninety per cent. serviceability throughout.

VIII

CHAMPIONS OF LIBERTY

For freedom's battle, once begun,
Bequeath'd by bleeding sire to son,
Though baffled oft, is ever won.

LORD BYRON.

CHAPTER VIII

CHAMPIONS OF LIBERTY

SOON after midday on D plus 6 (Monday, June 12th), a duck trundled up the wide sandy beach near Courseulles and came to a stop twenty yards short of the dunes. Just behind the driver there sat a broad-shouldered figure of a man. He wore a nautical peaked cap and smoked a cigar.

As soon as the duck was stationary he stood up and said, " How do I get out ? " and prepared to climb over the side and drop several feet to the ground.

A moment later, however, a soldier rushed up with a short ladder and Britain's Prime Minister made a more dignified descent on to liberated French soil than had at first seemed probable.

Mr. Churchill had previously leaned over the side of the duck to shake hands with another familiar figure who wore a short leather jacket, khaki corduroy trousers and a black beret with two badges.

Most remarkably, I was the only War Correspondent to witness this historic scene. A photographer raced up a few minutes after the duck had arrived on the beach and got a picture of Mr. Churchill as he moved off to a jeep drawn up near-by.

Word had come to the headquarters ship that " a distinguished personage " was to pay a visit and I had gone ashore early in the morning to search for the point of arrival. A long walk on the beaches had ended at a point about a quarter of a mile to the west of the little harbour of Courseulles.

I stopped to inquire of a major if he had any knowledge of a " visitor." " Well, apparently somebody is expected," said the major, pointing to a duck drawn up on the sands and facing out to sea about fifty yards away. No other vehicle was in the vicinity and there could be

no doubt that one of the two figures sitting in the duc
was that of the Commander-in-Chief of the Allied land forc

General Montgomery was using a pair of powerfu
binoculars to scan a wide sector of sea. The one youn
officer accompanying the General was also looking ou
to sea.

Satisfied that this was the point of arrival, althoug
there were no other indications such as Military Polic
or staff officers as one might have expected, I walke
along to a point immediately behind the Commander
in-Chief's duck. Some A.A. gunners were busy cleanin
their gun and only paused for a moment when I mentioned that General Montgomery was on the beach
near by.

These gunners had come in just after the first wave o
the assault. Fire from their anti-aircraft guns had swep
the beaches even as the battery prepared to go ashor
from the flat-bottomed craft taking them in. They ha
had a lot of work to do, especially at night, and expected
more. Their chief interest, apart from their guns, was
a stew with an appetising smell which was cooking on
an open fire a few yards away.

I sat on an iron beach obstruction which had been
pulled clear of the track running along the front of the
dunes above high-water mark, and waited. Forty yards
up the beach to the eastward a crippled L.C.T. lay aslant
across the beach. It looked as if its back was broken.
It rose up in the middle like some odd form of bridge
and the cabin at the stern of the craft might have been
a toll-house.

Closer to hand, in the fine, dry sand of the dunes,
there were many other indications of the battle that
had raged across this strip of shore less than a week
earlier. Odd bits of British and German equipment lay
half buried in the sand. Rubber life-belts, discarded by
the attackers, were tangled up with the gasmask equipment of the defenders. Empty British field-ration pack-
ages half covered ammunition clips dropped earlier.

Out at sea there was the grand panorama of ships.

Looked at from the low level of the beach, they appeared to go right over the horizon, and, because of the depth of the anchorage, there was hardly a clear patch of horizon to be seen.

Suddenly General Montgomery lowered his binoculars and swung himself out of the amphibious vehicle. The young staff officer was ahead of him and set off for the water's edge at the double, waving his arms as he went. A duck was coming along parallel with the beach and less than a hundred yards off-shore. As soon as the officer caught the attention of the driver the duck turned in and its slightly uneven movements made it clear that it had " touched down " and was coming up the sands on its wheels. General Montgomery walked towards it. With a sweep of his arm he indicated to the driver a course that would take him clear of a depression in the beach.

Then the duck stopped and the General, in two or three paces, was beside it and reaching up to grasp the extended hand of the Prime Minister.

I had followed the Commander-in-Chief down the beach and from close at hand saw the broad smile on Mr. Churchill's face. The other distinguished occupants of the duck were standing up. There was Field-Marshal Smuts, in a light khaki uniform, and Field-Marshal Sir Alan Brooke, Chief of the Imperial General Staff. In naval uniform there was Rear-Admiral Sir Philip Vian, in command of the eastern naval task force, and Commodore G. N. Oliver, in command of the naval forces in this sector of the beaches.

It was an historic moment, one felt, as the Prime Minister climbed over the side of the duck, slowly descended the ladder and set foot on the liberated soil of France. Without the courage and leadership of this man the Germans might well have been looking out to sea from that point, and looking without any immediate fears of invasion.

On the beach, Mr. Churchill looked around slowly, cigar in hand. Field-Marshal Smuts and the others followed him out of the duck. As they were being welcomed by General Montgomery, the Prime Minister, noticing my War Correspondent's badges, walked across and shook hands with me. I would have liked to have had a fine phrase ready to mark such an auspicious occasion, but, as is nearly always the case in such circumstances, I could think of nothing better to say than, "Good morning, sir," to which Mr. Churchill nodded rather solemnly, as if he felt it really was a *good* morning.

When Field-Marshal Smuts followed him I was ready with, "Welcome to France, sir." South Africa's world-famed statesman looked away across my shoulder and said quietly and movingly, "Yes, that is it—welcome to Free France."

Meanwhile, Mr. Churchill had settled himself comfortably in the back of a jeep which had been run down on to the sands. General Montgomery sat on the side of the vehicle, the better to talk with the Prime Minister and point out various things as they moved along. The two Field-Marshals got into another jeep.

A few military police had arrived on motor-cycles, and they completed the small procession that moved off towards a gap in the dunes.

It was apparent that word had gone round like lightning that Mr. Churchill had arrived on the beach. Excited soldiers and sailors were running along the sands waving and cheering. Mr. Churchill waved back. "Good old Winnie !" the fighting men shouted, and perhaps it was an amazed South African who started the cry of "Good old Jannie !"

There was a deep roar of cheering as Mr. Churchill gave his first "V" sign in France. As the jeeps swung through the gap in the dunes and out on to a dusty road, Spitfires raced overhead and naval guns, shelling the Germans far inland, boomed in what might have been taken for the Navy's own salute.

Following in the wake of the Prime Minister, I wondered if his eye had caught the red poppies still undisturbed in the fields fringed by the ugly skull and cross-bones mine warning signs left by the Germans.

Here again, in the first freed corner of France, were British soldiers amongst the poppies. Poignantly one remembered John McCrae's call from the last war :

> " Take up our quarrel with the foe :
> To you from failing hands we throw
> The torch ; be yours to hold it high.
> If ye break faith with us who die
> We shall not sleep, though poppies grow
> In Flanders fields."

And these men of a different generation who kept faith were, in many ways, so like their fathers. Sure of themselves and their cause, they still remained modest and unassuming. The most common reaction to the Prime Minister's visit was one of amazement that he should have thought fit to face the discomforts—and dangers—of what was still a forward area in order to see the fighting men. " Fancy him coming to see us," I heard men say over and over again.

Mr. Churchill was taken well inland, and as a result the Navy was not able to entertain him and the other visitors to a lunch on the beach. The naval Beach Master, ready for all emergencies, had " laid on " a meal of tinned steak and kidney pudding. Needless to say, such a luxury was not wasted, even though the Army had " bagged " the Prime Minister.

Later in the afternoon, as I left the beach at about the time Mr. Churchill was due to make his departure, the Luftwaffe made one of its rare daylight attacks. Four or five great spouts of water showed where the bombs had dropped harmlessly in the sea. Then the Spitfires, which had circled incessantly, got their sights on to the first enemy plane seen that day and the chase was on.

Word may have gone from one of the spies left behind by the Germans that the British Prime Minister had been in France, because the night that followed proved to be one of the noisiest we had experienced. After many warnings and much smoke, we lay down to sleep in our bunks in the *Hilary*. We were awakened by the repercussion of a heavy explosion and grabbed our life-belts and made for the deck in the belief that the ship had been hit.

Actually a bomb had dropped close enough to inflict slight damage on the *Hilary*—although even that was not discovered until the following day.

It was sufficient to disturb the Chief, who appeared, fully dressed, to comment in genuine, though comic, surprise, " The saucy so-and-so's ! "

Mr. Churchill made his return to England in the British destroyer *Kelvin*. His final words to the soldiers and sailors as he left France were, " God bless you and good luck to you."

It was the second day running that the *Kelvin* (Lieut.-Commander R. M. W. MacFarlan, R.N.) had found herself in the headlines. On the day before the Prime Minister's visit she flew the flag of the Allied Naval Commander-in-Chief when he crossed to France and met both Rear-Admiral Sir Philip Vian and Rear-Admiral Kirk. It was announced from Supreme Headquarters that Admiral Ramsay had expressed himself as " very satisfied with the development and progress made."

It was on the day that the Prime Minister passed safely to and from France that the Admiralty stated that a message congratulating all officers and men of H.M. Minesweeping forces for their continued success in destroying enemy mines had been conveyed by the First Lord of the Admiralty on behalf of the War Cabinet. " The message states," said the Admiralty, " that the War Cabinet fully appreciates that, but for the courage, skill and devotion of H.M. Minesweeping forces, the success of the recent amphibious operations, and especially of the landings in Normandy, could not have been achieved."

Lieut.-Commander Hugh Campbell, in command of the Canadian Fleet Sweeper *Fort William*, has written in verse of those days. With his permission I quote these stanzas :

" Great yarns are told of squadrons bold,
Of actions fought at sea.

> The River Plate, the *Scharnhorst's* fate,
>   Revenge and the Fifty-Three.
> And I propose to add to those
>   Exploits on the bounding billow,
> So lend an ear, and you shall hear
>   Of the Thirty-First M/S Flotilla.
>
> They had their chance, for off to France
>   The whole Flotilla sailed,
> One day in June, before the moon,
>   'Gainst morning's light had failed ;
> And far behind came every kind
>   Of craft that men could build,
> To take the ranks, the guns and tanks,—
>   And every craft was filled.
>
> For now at last, all waiting past,
>   This was the great occasion,
> The Thirty-First had been entrust
>   To spearhead the Invasion.
> That day, in light, and through the night,
>   They swept the channel clear,
> And with the dawn they still swept on—
>   The Norman coast was near.
>
> And week by week they hunt and seek
>   Those hornéd globes of hate.
> With little rest they give their best,
>   To keep an open gate.
> And every time they sink a mine,
>   Another victory's won ;
> The Nazi's grace, the Nazi's race,
>   Is that much nearer run."

Never was commendation better earned than by these
men of the sweeper flotillas.   With more and more ports
to sweep, in addition to their daily task on the supply
routes, their responsibilities increased as the weeks went
on, but they carried on with a determination and cheerfulness which was an example to all who came in contact
with them.

To mark the conclusion of the first week of the Invasion
there came, on D plus 7 (Tuesday, June 13th) a remarkable
tribute from Marshal Stalin.

The great leader of the Soviet has been a man of

remarkably few words, considering the position he holds
and his generous comment on the first seven day
following June 6th, 1944, should make it clear that he
at any rate, had a deep understanding of the test tha
faced the Allied forces when they approached Hitler'
citadel by sea and air from the west.

Said Marshal Stalin : " In summing up the results o
the seven days of battles of liberation by the Allie
troops who have invaded Northern France, one can sa
without hesitation that the large-scale forcing of th
Channel and the mass landing of troops of the Allie
in Northern France have fully succeeded. This is un
doubtedly a brilliant success for our Allies. One canno
but recognise that in the whole history of war there ha
not been any such undertaking so broad in conceptior
so grandiose in scale and so masterly in execution. A
is well known, the invincible Napoleon in his time ir
gloriously failed in his plan of crossing the Channel t
capture the British Isles. Hitler, the hysteric, who fc
years boasted that he would force the Channel, did nc
even risk making the attempt to carry out his threa
Only the British and American troops succeeded wit
honour in carrying out this immense plan of forcing th
Channel and landing troops on a vast scale. Histor
will record this as an achievement of the highest order.'

On D plus 8 (Wednesday, June 14th) I went in a
M.T.B. to visit the new " harbour " rapidly taking shap
in the sea off Port en Basin. Great hollow blocks o
concrete were still being towed from Britain to form th
outer protections of this pre-fabricated harbour. Man
had already settled on the bed of the sea and the fir
great right-angle of the sea wall was in place. Th
transfer of these blocks from England, where they we
assembled in various southern ports before the invasio
provided one of the largest towing undertakings ev
known. They had to be towed very slowly by powerful tug

Inside the breakwater were other specially designe
landing stages, capable of dealing with cargoes fro
ships at all states of the tide.

A " DUCK " TAKES THE SEA BY WAY OF THE LOWERED RAMP IN THE BOWS OF A TANK LANDING SHIP

(Crown copyright reserved)

NAVAL COMMANDO MEN SETTLE DOWN IN A BATTERED SECTION OF THE " IMPREGNABLE " WEST WALL

Two of these pre-fabricated harbours were designed long before the invasion, one for the British beaches and one for the Americans. Many difficulties had to be overcome. For some reason the War Office were given the job of making them.

Much later I heard on particularly good authority that when the Navy obtained information regarding the progress being made on the harbours, which came to be known as " Mulberries," they found that each section would take two and a half hours to sink, whereas the Navy said they must sink in a quarter of an hour.

Very great importance was attached to the Mulberries because they were expected to provide a sure landing in all weathers for at least a minimum of supplies for the troops put ashore in the early stages. A senior naval officer was placed in command of the whole organisation and the vast nature of it may be estimated from the fact that he eventually commanded 500 officers and 10,000 men.

He was certainly in command of the weirdest collection of floating things ever to come under the control of a British admiral. A " high-up " sailor, talking of them in the presence of Mr. Churchill in the days of their conception, unintentionally used the word " abortion," and I believe the term was not infrequently used by the Prime Minister himself when referring to them on subsequent occasions.

When the harbours were completed, Liberty ships and coasters were able to go alongside the piers. The great and almost unprecedented summer gale that hit the anchorage less than a fortnight after the initial landings, might have had disastrous results but for the protection afforded to shipping by the two forms of artificial harbour set down by the Allies.

The storm, in fact, did lead to disaster as far as the American Mulberry was concerned. It failed to withstand the battering of the sea and was of little use subsequently.

The British Mulberry was more fortunate and was a

great success. Designed to handle 3,000 tons of supplies a day, it actually touched the remarkable total of 9,000 tons on at least one occasion. One officer said of it : ".From the air it looks as good as Portland harbour."

The American Mulberry had the misfortune to be in a more exposed position than the British harbour and the violent four-day gale broke it up, although each of the concrete sections displaced over 6,000 tons.

A big bluff was worked on the Germans when the sections were assembled before June 6th. Some were built into the shape of a small harbour at Dungeness while others were got together off Selsey Bill. Built on the Thames and around the Solent, there were something like 150 of them, and they presented a most curious sight. It was impossible to hide them from the enemy, but they were so placed as to leave him with the impression that they might be used in the Pas de Calais area. In this way they were possibly responsible for a measure of the surprise that went with the attack on the Normandy beaches.

An official account dealing with the prefabricated harbours, which was issued more than four months after D Day, gave these interesting details :

In order to accommodate the necessary shipping and port equipment the size of each harbour had to be roughly the same as Dover, which entailed the construction of 150 caissons.

It was a British responsibility to provide and deliver all the equipment necessary at the far shore for both harbours. The construction of the American harbour was the responsibility of the United States Navy, while that of the British harbour was combined Royal Navy and Army.

The total tug fleet available for towing the equipment was 85, varying from very large United States tugs of over 1,500 h.p. to small tugs of 600 h.p. not generally used in the open sea.

A minimum of 210 tows was required, involving a weight of over 1,000,000 tons, allowing for few losses by enemy action, and each round trip was expected to take three days. Luckily there were very few losses of tugs, and they carried out this unusual, strenuous and sometimes dangerous task with great patience, courage and skill.

In the setting down of the harbour the Navy and Army worked hand in hand ; soldiers were sailors and sailors were soldiers, and Royal Marines were both. This operation was half finished by D-plus-12, by which time one pier hundreds of yards long with several pier heads was complete, and coasters could be unloaded at any state of the tide.

But on D-plus-13 a gale blew up from the north-east which continued for three days, the worst June gale experienced for 40 years. Moreover, it came from the worst possible direction and the harbours were exposed to its full force. Unfortunately it caught the harbours at the halfway stage.

The American harbour suffered most severely, as it was in a more exposed site, and the breakwaters were largely broken up, so much so that this, combined with the capture of Cherbourg, caused the work on this harbour to be discontinued.

The British harbour was protected to some extent by the Calvados reef, and suffered far less damage, from which it was soon able to recover and be completed.

An appendix to the official account stated that each caisson contained crews' quarters for use during the passage, the crew being partly naval for handling the ship and partly from Royal Engineers (or Seabees) for carrying out the operation of sinking. At a late stage Bofors guns, twenty tons of ammunition and rough shelters for a gun's crew were placed on the top of most caissons as additional A.A. protection of the harbour. The total labour forces involved in the construction, which does not include the fabrication of many essential small parts, was about 20,000 men. This included 1,200 skilled fitters, 1,400 carpenters, and 2,400 semi-skilled workers, all of whom had to be mobilised and moved to the right areas by the Ministry of Labour.

From the deck of the *Hilary* on the evening of D plus 8 we witnessed one of the most spectacular air attacks of the war. While it was still daylight, wave after wave of Lancasters flew over and dropped their heavy loads of bombs on the E-boat pens, the docks and the German guns in Le Havre. They were part of a force of more than 1,100 heavy bombers sent out over a period of a few hours. Intense flak had to be faced, but the bombers went straight in to their targets and the roar and vibration of their bombs could be heard and felt miles away at sea. Twelve thousand pound block-busters were used and the total weight of bombs probably exceeded 1,500 tons.

It was an impressive display of air power and, once again, we in the ships in the anchorage thanked our stars that air supremacy rested with the Allies.

While the bombs went down, British naval forces waited outside Le Havre to intercept any ships that might try to " run for it." Nothing came out, however. Two hours later, after darkness had fallen, Le Havre had another visitation from Allied air forces.

The effect of these raids could only be fully estimated after air photographs had been taken some hours later. They showed that the largest concentration of E and R-boats in the harbour, which were at their moorings along the quayside to the north of the Basin de Maree, had been sunk. Vessels, including torpedo-boats, at the side of the deep-water quay near the passenger railway station and at the end of the north quay, were also sunk. One of these torpedo-boats was still burning fiercely when the first set of air photographs was taken. Later in the day it had disappeared.

It was claimed that the 12,000-lb. bombs dropped would have raised a tidal wave when they burst in the water that would have swept into the pens and undermined their structure. The photographs showed that one E-boat had been thrown up on to a bank in a damaged condition by this wave. The pens themselves were hit by heavy bombs. A large floating dock was also sunk and there was extensive damage to quayside buildings. In the maritime station, close to which the E-boats were moored, a huge explosion swept away all the buildings and left a clear space 150 yards across.

The S.H.A.E.F. Communiqué for the same day recorded that enemy mobile batteries on the flanks of our forces were engaged by Allied warships. On the eastern flank H.M.S. *Belfast* (Captain F. R. Parham, D.S.O., R.N.) wearing the flag of Vice-Admiral F. H. G. Dalrymple-Hamilton, C.B., gave valuable support against enemy concentrations. H.M.S. *Nelson* (Captain A. H. Maxwell-Hyslop, A.M., R.N.) engaged the batteries of Le Havre.

It was further stated that during an unsuccessful enemy air attack in the western assault area an enemy aircraft was shot down by the U.S.S. *Augusta* (Captain E. H. Jones, U.S.N.) wearing the flag of Rear Admiral Alan Goodrich Kirk, U.S.N.

" Convoys of Allied merchant ships are arriving satisfactorily and the armies continue to be built up with men, stores and equipment," the communiqué ended.

In fact, everything seemed pretty satisfactory after eight days' hard fighting.

This time, too, was marked by another memorable visit—that of General de Gaulle, leader of the Free French. He came in the French destroyer *Combattante*, and went ashore in a duck, as Mr. Churchill had done, two days earlier.

There was no mistaking the tall figure, wearing a long khaki overcoat and the familiar high French cap. At the point where the General got into a jeep, a piece of wood had been nailed to an upturned rifle stuck in the sandy soil. On the wood was roughly written : " Here lies a Canadian soldier."

The General was obviously keeping a tight hold on his feelings. The only words he had said as he looked towards the coast of France on the way in were, " After five years." But for a man whose record shows that he places France before everything else in the world, it must have been a profoundly moving moment.

Other officers with the General could not hide their feelings. I joined the small procession in which they drove to General Montgomery's headquarters. The officers waved and the French people in the villages could not believe their eyes. Their mouths opened, sometimes forming the one word " de Gaulle," and then they were left standing by the roadside. One old man who touched his cap to the people in the fast-moving cars out of habit, suddenly recognised the General. He dropped a parcel he was carrying and ran into the middle of the road as the cars went by in a cloud of dust. When we last saw him he was dancing with delight.

But among all these stirring and encouraging events there were plenty of signs that the Germans had not completely shot their bolt and not one man in the Allied navies was working on the assumption that they had. It was on D plus 9 (Thursday, June 15th), that Admiral Ramsay told my colleague, Leslie Randall, that the Germans were bringing up their E boats. " When we first went over we caught them on the hop," he said. " They were in port because they could not be out all the time on account of the strain on their crews. But now they are coming out. They come out at night and if they got through to our convoys they would cause frightful damage. Our light coastal forces and destroyers are fighting them all the time. They are simply grand. They are doing the biggest job of all."

The " little ships " fought as many as seven actions a night. They were hard fights, often against heavy odds and in one of them Arthur Thorpe, naval correspondent of the Exchange Telegraph Company, was killed. Thorpe had seen much of the war and had survived the sinking of two aircraft-carriers, the *Ark Royal* and the *Eagle*. Hearing the sad news over the radio in H.M.S. *Hilary* one night, I remembered the many occasions when Thorpe and I had worked together before the war and I knew that many Fleet street men would feel as I felt, that one of the straightest men ever to engage in " the newspaper game " had given his life while covering the greatest assignment of all.

Here is the story of a single action in which one M.L. fought off ten German E boats that were attempting to attack a convoy of landing craft crossing to Normandy : At about 4 a.m., when the convoy was in mid-Channel, the M.L., which was commanded by Lieut. J. C. Lewis, heard firing to the eastward. Five minutes later two E boats were seen about 600 yards away.

" We closed the range and opened fire with our Oerlikons and machine-guns," said Lieut. B. K. C. Arbuthnot, R.N., who was on board the M.L. " The E boats gave us a parting shot as they scuttled away. My experience has been that E boats are shy of returning fire. A minute later we turned our fire against new antagonists. That lot disappeared in a smoke-screen, but E boats appeared to be everywhere. We got in close to the convoy to protect it. We were immediately engaged by more E boats and one was sighted about five hundred yards to port. We turned to engage this one and a very hot duel ensued, during which we sustained most of our damage. One shell hit our smoke-container and we were soon emitting an involuntary smoke-screen. At first we thought the ship was on fire. More engagements followed at longer range, until the Germans retired at dawn. The E boats used flares and starshells to silhouette our convoy, but these proved a double edged weapon. The landing craft put up a fierce fire whenever they saw a target."

Although the series of one-sided actions lasted for one hour and forty-five minutes, all but two of the landing craft got through safely.

The " little ships," fighting on the fringes of the anchorages, protected not only the supply ships but the larger warships, still engaged in shelling the German positions inland.

D plus 9 was a day of heavy bombardments in which both British and U.S. battleships joined. H.M.S.

Ramillies (Captain G. B. Middleton, C.B.E., R.N.) engaged a battery at Benerville on our eastern flank. Ship
and land guns fought it out for an hour, after which
there was no more firing from the German battery. The
Nelson, with her sixteen inch guns, plastered an enemy
battery north of Le Havre, which had been dropping
shells in the anchorage. On the western flank the
U.S.S. *Texas* (Captain C. A. Baker, U.S.N.) wearing the
flag of Rear Admiral K. Carleton F. Bryant, U.S.N.,
the U.S.S. *Nevada* (Captain P. M. Rhea, U.S.N.) and the
U.S.S. *Arkansas* (Captain F. G. Richards, U.S.N.)
carried out heavy bombardments in support of the
armies near Isigny and Carentan.

The British cruiser *Arethusa* steamed into the anchorage
on the morning of D plus 10 (Friday, June 16th) but, at
the time, only a handful of the thousands of sailors and
soldiers in the vicinity knew that she had brought the
most distinguished visitor of all to Normandy—His
Majesty the King.

The weather had definitely broken and a stiff wind
was sending the low clouds scudding across the sky and
tipping the waves with white horses. The little boats,
so essential to the anchorage, were having a rough time,
but nobody thought of running for cover—unless a boat
was so full of water that she was liable to sink at any
minute.

From the bridge-house roof of one of the old freighters
sunk to form the Gooseberry (which was about to prove
its usefulness to the full) I had a grandstand view of the
King's arrival in the midst of the Invasion fleet.

The *Arethusa* came in, escorted by two destroyers, and
dropped anchor not far from the cruiser *Scylla*, Admiral
Vian's flagship. An M.T.B. raced towards her and the
King, in naval uniform, wasted no time in getting aboard.

The Navy is intensely proud of the fact that the King
has served in the Navy in peace and war. Officers and
ratings always speak of the King as one of themselves.
They notice the little things that speak of his naval
training. Not keeping a boat waiting alongside a ship

in rough weather was just one of these things. Long-service Petty Officers nodded their heads in respectful approval and commented, " Bet he'd sooner stay with us than go around them dusty roads ! "

The King was brought ashore through the mass of shipping in the M.T.B. The graceful bows cut a clean course through the sea but occasionally spray slashed across the low bridge where the King stood.

The craft carried the Royal Standard. I was relieved to see it because I knew what consternation had been caused only a few hours before when it was discovered that there was not a Standard to be found among all the ships of the Fleet in the anchorage—they had all been taken away at the beginning of the war.

The Navy, used to overcoming all forms of difficulties, decided that a Royal Standard must be made forthwith. But neither yellow bunting nor yellow paint was available. Undaunted, the Signals branch mixed a large jar of mustard and applied it in a thick coat.

Many small craft were inside the protecting barrier of old tramp ships and they could know nothing of the King's approach until the M.T.B. swung round the end of the Gooseberry. One of the first vessels to meet the royal boat was an L.C.I., heading out to sea. Very smartly the young Commanding Officer mustered half a dozen of his small crew. They stood rigidly to attention on the swaying deck while their officer saluted. Some of them had grimy faces and their uniforms fell far short of review standards but the King was quick to acknowledge their salute.

In the shelter of the Gooseberry the King transferred from the M.T.B. to the ubiquitous duck and slowly started on the last lap for the shore. He was not many yards from the ugly L.C.K., but the cooks, hard at work in the smoking galleys, probably did not know that the King had looked upon their useful craft. Many of the sailors did hear that the King was among them and came tumbling up on deck, eager to cheer.

After several hours ashore with the army, the King

re-embarked in the *Arethusa* and made a safe return to England.

Very early next morning I followed him across the Channel in a famous fighting destroyer, the *Jervis*. She had been on patrol all night and slipped in to pick up one or two " passengers " before racing back to England.

I said " Good bye " to *Hilary*, and the cheerful, courageous company in which I had lived for a memorable fortnight, with very real regret. Throughout that time, whatever the immediate difficulties or dangers, I received nothing but the most courteous and helpful treatment from every officer and man in the ship.

In *Jervis* we made a very quick return to England, disposing of an excellent breakfast and three mines on the way. The mines, fortunately, went off far behind our wake.

Later I received this letter from the Wardroom Mess of the *Jervis*, which I set on record as typical of the unfailing good humour of the Navy :

" DEAR SIR—We have just received a letter from the Press Division of the Admiralty stating that they are charging you with the sum of 5s. 6d. for one somewhat doubtful breakfast on passage from Normandy to the United Kingdom. We feel that such a price is heavy even for the pleasure of our company and we are therefore returning this sum on receipt of same. Lest you should think that we are unprincipled robbers, we would plead in our defence that robbers we may be —but not unprincipled. We have a heavy Mess debt and take every chance of extracting money from sources which we consider will not notice the loss. Thus, in your case, we believed we were drawing on the funds of the Press Division and not on your own private means. Please accept our apologies in this matter and pay us a visit on every opportunity you may have."

IX

BY LAND, SEA AND AIR

For while the tired waves, vainly breaking,
Seem here no painful inch to gain,
Far back, through creeks and inlets making,
Comes silent, flooding in, the main.

A. H. CLOUGH.

IX

BY LAND, SEA AND AIR

IN the course of its manifold activities, the Navy took to
the land in the early stages of the invasion. An R.N.
and Royal Marine Commando engaged in a number of
astonishing exploits which I am not in a position to
describe in detail at this stage.

They were in the middle of one of their " private
battles " when I had the pleasure of meeting Commander
Dunstan Curtis, who commanded the motor gunboat
that led the *Campbeltown* into St. Nazaire on the occasion
of the famous raid.

The Commander, with his trim reddish beard, had tired
of taking Commando men on expeditions and had himself
become a leader of a special service group. Not everybody would have been encouraged to join a Commando
by the experiences of St. Nazaire.

With amusing detachment, over a drink in the ward-
room, he told me that his men were " sitting on top of
the Germans " in an enemy strong-point which had held
out after our line had swept several miles inland. The
Germans were able to hold out because they were deep
underground and their " fort " was faced with solid rock.

The strong-point was in the region of Douvres. The
naval Commando had arrived on the scene and, in
co-operation with an army battalion, proposed to shift
the enemy. The garrison, however, were so unaggressive,
and imposed so little inconvenience on the army using
roads quite close to them, that it was decided that there
was no need to risk heavy casualties in assaulting the
concrete, mine-encircled defences.

So the Commando men settled down to a cat and
mouse game, with the German garrison very much the
mouse. A château, which was previously occupied by
the Germans, was taken over by them. " I believe the

German commander can see me having dinner in the room he used to eat in," said Commander Curtis.

Little trouble came from the Germans and even at night they did no more than indulge in sniping. A report came from the French people in the neighbourhood that the senior German officer was seen out on a bicycle one night. He had lived in the district a long time and knew the paths and by-lanes. He also knew how to get back home quickly when the Commando men started looking for him.

The end came after twelve days when, under cover of gunfire from a few tanks, the Commando men attacked the strong-point. It was still a formidable objective but the Germans had not much fight left in them and the point was taken with only slight casualties to the sailors and marines.

A Royal Marine officer's comment afterwards was, " We marched round and round the place, like Joshua round Jericho. Then, when we were ready, we blew our trumpets and the walls fell down."

Before surrendering, the garrison played one typical Nazi trick. Five men emerged from the subterranean defences with their hands up. They also carried a white flag, and a tank officer climbed out to accept their surrender. The leading German threw a grenade in his face, killing him. Immediately the five Germans were mown down and the remainder of the garrison tumbled over themselves to make a genuine surrender.

This was but one instance of the Navy giving direct assistance to the Army. There were many such cases of inter-service aid. The Army and R.A.F., for instance, had their own recovery units for getting in equipment that had been caught by the tide on the beaches. Tanks, bulldozers, jeeps and motor-cycles were among the vehicles which eventually headed into France, although they had spent hours and sometimes days under water before getting ashore.

The R.A.F., in a final assessment of " aid rendered " in the bombing attacks on Le Havre and Boulogne on

June 14th and 15th, claimed eighty vessels. The total was made up of twenty-two E and R boats, three torpedo-boats, one corvette, one M class sweeper, three M class tenders, six tank landing craft, a score of naval auxiliaries and another score of vessels of various types.

A fine example of the appreciation felt by one Service for another was given by Group Captain R. Cleland, R.A.F., who was directing R.A.F. support from the anchorage from D day until the establishment of air-fields in France. " I have seen the Royal Navy at close quarters," he said, on his return to Britain, " and in my opinion it was primarily due to the crews who handled the landing craft, plying between the transport and the beaches, that the bridgehead was so successfully estab-lished. The sea conditions were difficult. In fact, had they been one degree worse it might have been impossible to carry out the landings. Yet these sailors handled their craft with their heavy loads of men and material with superb skill. Every landing craft, so far as I know, was commanded either by a lieutenant or sub-lieutenant of the R.N.V.R., and the vast majority of the crews came from civilian jobs which had not the remotest connection with seafaring. What it is, in the British navy, that makes competent seamen out of such material in so short a time beats me. They had the responsibility of getting the troops ashore in a condition fit to fight. Weaving a way through the maze of mines and beach obstacles which lay thick in the water close to the beach, with heavy swell trying to take control of the craft, demanded nerve, coolness and skilled seamanship. These boys—' amateur sailors ' they used to call them—had all these things. The most difficult part for them was the return from the beaches. It was impossible for the crews to exercise full control as they manœuvred their craft stern first away from the beaches. The swell caught the craft beam on and swung some of them on to the mines. In this way some of the crews lost their lives. There was a lot of sniping going on around the beaches for the first few days but nobody appeared to pay much attention. They were too busy with the job of unloading troops and materials and getting them off to the front line. Busiest man of all was the burly, bearded figure of Captain C. D. Maud, D.S.O., D.S.C., R.N., striding along the beaches armed with a fearsome looking cudgel, directing landing operations. Since D day he has been naval officer in charge of captured enemy beaches over an area five miles in width and, despite the tremendous traffic of men and materials continuously arriving from the sea, he seemed to have everything going like clock-work. He was the station master of one of the biggest termini of all times—created within a few hours from a mined and bullet-spattered stretch of sand. The way Commodore Oliver organised the flow of troops and materials from the transports and the way Captain Maud organised the receiving of them, earned a special message of congratulation from Rear Admiral Sir Philip Vian on board his flagship, the cruiser *Scylla*."

No compliment could have been more handsome, as paid by a senior officer of one Service to the officers and men of another.

The Americans, too, were generous in their praise of the efforts of the Royal Navy. " I wish you could see what your gunfire has done. It has smashed up some terrific emplacements," was a signal sent by a senior American army officer to H.M.S. *Black Prince* (Captain D. M. Lees, D.S.O., R.N.). The British cruiser was operating with a U.S. squadron and, for ten days, pin-pointed targets at the request of U.S. land forces pushing the Germans back from the sea. Of thirty-five specially indicated targets she destroyed twenty for certain. Targets ranged from beach pill-boxes, machine-gun nests in houses and infantry hiding in woods to howitzers, 88 mm. and other heavy artillery. The first target, a howitzer battery, was knocked out in less than half an hour.

Lieut. Commander C. Le M. Scott, R.N., of Uckfield, Sussex, Gunnery officer of *Black Prince*, was inclined to think the shooting dull. " Most of the time we were

THE TANKS COME ASHORE THROUGH THE JAWS OF THE L.S.T.'s

(Royal Canadian Navy Photograph)

H.M.S. "ENTERPRISE" STEAMS INTO A SMOKE SCREEN LAID BY A U.S. DESTROYER DURING THE
BOMBARDMENT OF CHERBOURG

firing at map references and could not see what our shells were doing," he said afterwards. "Our rate of firing was a good deal slower than it would have been in a sea action."

The brief entries in the Gunnery Log reflected the almost routine nature of the firing. Here are typical entries : " Pill boxes on beach—twelve direct hits," and " Beach defences. Machine-guns firing at troops—neutralised." In the results column two words were frequently repeated—" Fire effective."

For the first thirty-six hours the ship's company remained at action stations but as it became apparent that the Germans were in no position to counter attack heavily, either by sea or air, this was relaxed. Sandwiches and tea were served to begin with to the men as they still manned the guns. Later a hot meal service was organised and many of the crew were able to sleep, lying on deck in the sunshine.

Commander R. A. V. Gregory, R.N., speaking of the scene, declared that salvoes from the guns did not make the sleepers even twitch.

There was one shore battery which occasionally opened up on the cruiser. "It did not worry us much," said Lieut. Commander Scott. "Whenever we had nothing more important to do we took pot shots at it and eventually it was silenced."

Another target for the *Black Prince* was an observation post in the vicinity of Montebourg. They had a double crack at it. Having closed it down overnight, the army asked the cruiser to repeat the operation early next morning. They did not have to ask a third time, a direct hit being scored with the first morning salvo.

H.M.S. *Tyler* (Lieut. C. H. Rankin, R.N.), a Captain-class frigate, did not even enjoy an early bombardment of the Hun positions. She was on escort duty, and no German targets could be found to test the gunners, who had half imagined they would find themselves in a big sea battle.

Nobody was more disappointed than Sub-Lieut. D.

Gibson, R.N.V.R., an American from Pittsburg, Pennsylvania, who joined the Royal Navy because he wanted " to have a crack at the Nazis and could not wait until the United States entered the war."

" As we set off on our first trip across the Channel, I thought this was the big moment," he said.   " But all I got was a grandstand view of the launching of the Second Front.   The sight of 4,000 ships of all shapes and sizes coming and going between England and France was hard to believe.   I would not have believed such an armada possible unless I had seen it myself.   It did me good, as an American, to see so many Liberty ships in that solid mass of shipping.   But the thing that impresed me most was the sight, through binoculars, of a party of Royal Marines playing darts on the deck of the cruiser *Belfast* as she was firing salvo after salvo on to the enemy coast ! "

Although the main part of the Invasion armada was British and American, the other Allied navies made their contribution, as they have done all along.

Among the Dutch ships were two gunboats, the *Soemba* and *Flores*.   Sister ships, they were split up for the invasion, *Soemba* being attached to the Americans and *Flores* to the British.

Soemba went to the French coast escorting a convoy. She then took part in the bombardment of enemy positions.   Having smashed up batteries near Isigny, *Soemba* went off to support American forces near St. Marcouf, where the most accurate shooting was necessary as the land forces were very close to each other.

The shooting was not all one-sided and the *Soemba* had a narrow escape from one German salvo, which landed where she had been at anchor only a few minutes earlier.   On another occasion she was going astern across a sandbank when minesweepers blew up two mines immediately in her track, while, to make things more difficult, an escaped barrage balloon entangled itself in her mast.

Going to relieve the *Flores*, who had worn out her second set of guns by continuous shooting, *Soemba* received a warm welcome from many old friends from the Mediterranean, including a British cruiser and armed merchantmen with whom she had engaged on anti-submarine patrol in the Persian Gulf. The British naval commander in this section found plenty of work for the Dutch gunboat and she helped to shake up the Germans to the east of the River Orne. The Dutch sailors were highly pleased with one of the air observers who found plenty of targets for them. Once he signalled, " Sorry to keep you waiting, but I am under fire myself ! "

The words of a senior staff officer of the Royal Artillery prove that the *Flores* was just as successful. " A little gunboat, the *Flores*, manned by a Dutch crew, went straight in in a most audacious fashion and wiped out a battery which, had it not been rendered ineffective, might have had disastrous consequences for the beach invaders," he said. " Four squadrons of heavy bombers had tried to knock the battery out, but failed, and it was then the *Flores* took on the target. She went in and did the job single-handed."

The Netherlands naval contribution in the six weeks following the Invasion included nine trips to France by the *Mecklenburg*, during which 6,000 British and American troops were carried ; six trips by the *Batavier II* to bring back 1,300 wounded men from France ; an average of four trips each by coasters, carrying a total of 81,000 tons of war material ; many operational trips by M.T.B.'s.

During one of the latter, three enemy E-boats were sighted at night, south of Cape Gris Nez. They were engaged by the patrol force commanded by Lieut. W. A. Delooze, D.S.C., R.N.N., and made off inshore under cover of smoke. Turning to the eastward, Lieut. Delooze found two groups of armed trawlers. Starshells from shore batteries lit up his force and there was heavy fire from the trawlers, but hits were observed on the German vessels before Lieut. Delooze withdrew.

An ordinary seaman of an M.T.B. flotilla received the Dutch Cross of Merit for his courage after his craft had struck a mine off the French coast. The seaman was

below decks when the mine exploded, and suffered from
shock and a wound on the head.   He not only got clear
of the badly-damaged boat, but also helped to drag
three men from the engine-room.

Units of the Free French Navy which took part in the
initial attack came within sight of France without being
able to go ashore.   The ships included *La Surprise*
(Captain Lavasseur), *L'Adventure* (Captain Querville), *La
Decouverte* (Captain Recher), *L'Escarmouche* (Captain de
Lesquien), *Aconit* (Captain le Millier), *Renoncule* (Lieut.
Mithois), *Rosalies* (Captain Kolb Bernard) and *D'Estienne
d'Orves* (Captain Sabouret).

Captain Levasseur, who once sank two U-boats in
ten hours in the Atlantic, told me how he called the
crew of *La Surprise* together on the quarter-deck ten
minutes before the frigate sailed on the eve of D Day.
" The hour for which you have waited so long has come,"
he said.   " We sail with the Allied Armies for France ! "
The ship's company was still cheering when they put to sea.

The crews of the French ships knew that there was
work to be done and that they would not get ashore,
so they flew the largest tricolours they could find, and
went as close inshore as they dared, in the hope that
their countrymen would see the flag of France in the
great mass of shipping.

The destroyer *Combattante* was in the protecting force
when French Commandos landed.   The Fusiliers-Marins
Commandos had the honor on D Day of being the first
Commandos to leap ashore in their sector.   They stormed
their first objective under heavy fire and in six hour
advanced nearly seven miles.   For thirteen days they
remained in the thick of the fight, never losing contact
with the enemy.

The General commanding the Brigade sent this message
to their Commanding Officer : " I thank and congratulate
you on the magnificent fighting qualities of the troop
you command.   I can only remind you of the word
taken from your own language, that belong to history
' Sans peur et sans reproche.' "

Polish and Norwegian ships were fighting off the beaches from the earliest stages of the Invasion and the Royal Norwegian Navy suffered the loss of the destroyer *Svenner*.

Our own losses, as announced by the Admiralty on July 13th, 1944, were :

The destroyers :

H.M.S. *Boadicea* (Lieut-.Commander F. W. Hawkins, R.N.).

H.M.S. *Swift* (Lieut.-Commander J. R. Gower, R.N.).

The frigates :

H.M.S. *Mourne* (Lieut.-Commander R. S. Holland, R.D., R.N.R.).

H.M.S. *Blackwood* (Lieut.-Commander L. T. Sly, R.D., R.N.R.).

H.M.S. *Lawford* (Lieut.-Commander M. C. Morris, R.N.).

The trawler :

H.M.S. *Lord Austin* (Lieut. E. S. T. Robinson, R.N.V.R.).

The auxiliary :

H.M.S. *Minster* (Acting Lieut.-Commander W. Jackson, R.N.R.)

Several smaller units had also been sunk up to that time, but the list, in view of the magnitude of the operation, was unbelievably short.

Even in the face of disaster, Allied naval men sometimes found a laugh. One small craft was sunk just before H hour and the crew were left tossing about in a rubber raft a mile or so from the shore. A youthful officer asked for permission to swim ashore. It was given, and he plunged into the sea and swam strongly for the beach. He reached it only a little behind the assault craft and found himself under heavy fire. He made a dash to a group of landing craft, got a " lift " in an L.C.V.P. and was back on board a transport long before his shipmates were picked up.

One young sailor was in the crow's-nest of a ship when a shell went right through the mast. The sailor disappeared in the sea and later the ship sank. Survivors going on board a transport were amazed to find that their comrade who had been flung out of the crow's-nest was already there.

Another sailor who was flung into the sea came up and scrambled on to something in the water. He made frantic signals for help, but the vessels on the way to the beach could not stop. He had a life-jacket and appeared to be well supported. His urgent desire to be picked up was explained when a ship approached and the sailor shouted a warning. " I am sitting on a mine ! " he said.

A little heartless, perhaps, but still amusing, is the story of the airman on a rubber raft in the water. He was attempting to signal with a flash-lamp. A signal rating in an American ship studied the flashes for a while and then reported to the bridge, " There's a guy out there calling for his mother. He keeps sending M.O.M., M.O.M., M.O.M."

Typical of the determination shown by navy men in the face of misfortune is the story of L.C.T. 593. One hour and forty minutes after H hour, 593 ran full speed on to the beach not far from Ouistreham. She carried four self-propelled guns, three Sherman tanks, four half-track vehicles and eighty soldiers. They all got ashore in less than two feet of water. But the L.C.T. had been holed in several places by the jagged beach obstacles. Efforts were made to plug the holes, 140 blankets being used, among other things. With the pumps going, the L.C.T. got off. Then the engines failed and the craft threatened to sink in a matter of minutes. Her commanding officer, Lieut. J. F. D. E. Jones, R.N.V.R., just managed to get her back on the beach. There would have been every justification for abandoning the vessel, especially as she was under German fire. But Lieut. Jones and his crew had other ideas. German aircraft came to bomb them, but they manned the guns and drove the planes off. Then German snipers tried to pick off the crew, and the ship's guns were turned on buildings along the shore. The crew of 593 were out to save their vessel. Leading Seaman Lawton, a Cornishman from Penzance, stuck to his gun for seventeen hours, and then only left it on orders. The guns were constantly manned for three days and nights. At dawn on D plus One, six Junkers 88's came over and bombs were dropped all around the stranded landing craft. Ordinary Seaman S. Townsend, from Beccles, Suffolk, got a hit on one of the aircraft and set its starboard engine on fire. Three of the crew and two of a party of salvage-men who had arrived were wounded. Stoker Tom Beatson, of Sheffield, died later from his wounds. Still the gallant crew hung on, working all the time to patch up their craft. Eventually the repairs had gone far enough to enable her to be towed off and on D plus Six the 593 arrived back in England.

Many damaged craft were returned to service, and Wrens, who contributed so splendidly in many fields to the success of the Invasion, helped to repair them. Qualified Maintenance Wrens, working in blue overalls and navy caps, attended to gun mountings and other important parts of the ships. Electrical Maintenance Wrens made the intricate wiring systems function again and Supply Wrens issued the victuals for the vessels. Girl drivers, too, brought the vehicles alongside in which supplies and replacements came.

In floating docks Wrens proved themselves fine hands at scraping, cleaning and painting craft. In workshops they were ready for the toughest jobs. A Wren moulder's mate, for instance, would help to cast a new propeller. These girls, of whom the Navy is very rightly proud, took night-work in their stride. No task was too big or too small for them. Letters from the Fleet Mail office reached the men returning from the other side through Wrens, and survivors got food and clothing from the girls in navy blue.

Their work in the signal section was outstanding and received the personal approbation of Admiral Ramsay. They were entrusted with many secrets of the highest order and their integrity was equal to their efficiency.

" A quick turn-round and a high maintenance of serviceability remains our aim until the Army has finally overcome all resistance in the West," said the Allied Naval Commander-in-Chief in a message to all landing ships, landing craft and barge crews towards the end of July.

In congratulating them on their " efficiency and cheerfulness so often under adverse weather conditions," Admiral Ramsay added, " The build-up period lacks the excitement of the initial assaults and indeed the spur of anticipation of the pre-D Day training period, but it is none the less of vital and continued importance.

Officers and men responded with enthusiasm. A few days later I went on board L.S.T. 425 (Commander C. M. V. Dalrymple-Hay) when she was about to set off on her twenty-first trip to France. I found that in less than two months this one ship had carried 1,222 vehicles, 221 officers and 3,740 other ranks across the Channel. Among the units she helped to " lift " were the 7th Canadian Infantry Brigade, Royal Armoured Corps, Royal Corps of Signals, 70th U.S. Tank Battalion, Field Artillery, a Group, R.A.F., 49th Infantry Brigade, R.A.S.C., R.E.M.E., Corps of Military Police, U.S. Army Field Engineers and a Polish Field Regiment.

On one trip they returned with 1,100 German prisoners.

The full record of L.S.T. 425 offered impressive proof of the value of these ships, without which the invasion of Europe might not have been a practical proposition.

Built almost completely by women in a Baltimore yard, she was commissioned and brought across the Atlantic by the Royal Navy eighteen months before we went into France. In that time she engaged in four major landing operations—at Reggio, Salerno, Ajaccio and Anzio.

Before her ramp ever touched the Normandy beaches she had carried 10,000 officers and men—British, American and Free French—to begin the process of cleaning up Europe. Her total of fighting vehicles carried had reached 1,800.

It was not surprising that when D Day came the men

of L.S.T. 425 should count it routine work. On one of
their early trips they made goal-posts out of bundles of
clothes and played a football match with L.S.T. 415
on the beaches where the Germans had thought to bar
our way into France.

I have referred before to the hard fighting that our
Light Coastal Forces and their American counterpart were
called upon to do. As time went by, at any rate up to
the end of the first two months or more, this was in-
tensified. The Germans congregated in Le Havre and
developed fresh tactics for attacking our shipping. New
weapons, such as the human torpedo and explosive
motor-boat, were introduced and the "little ships"
were in the front line against them.

Soon after D Day the enemy used his high-powered
and heavily-armed craft to attack from both east and
west. Cherbourg was the western lair for his boats and
the threat was a considerable one. But after several
rough handlings by our M.T.B.'s the Germans withdrew
their vessels from Cherbourg, although the port was still
in their hands.

The young men of Coastal Forces, who have had as
tough a time as any fighting men in this war, went all
out for the enemy. After five years of war we were
still not over-stocked with M.T.B. flotillas, and the
Germans still had certain advantages in their boats, such
as Diesel engines, which were, in the estimation of many
of those serving in Coastal Forces, much better suited
to the needs of this type of warfare than the engines
fitted in our own boats. To meet and hold the Hun
therefore called for a great effort on the part of the existing flotillas. Fortunately there were still men whose
calibre reached up to that of the late Lieut.-Commander
Robert Hichins, the Cornish solicitor, whose inspired
leadership set the standard for our little ships.

Lieut. Dudley Dixon, R.N.V.R., for instance, served
under "Hich" and now, leading a flotilla himself, was
prepared to fight with the same determination and skill.
Indeed, it was only determination that carried him into

the battle at all because he was in hospital with a nasty wound in the leg until just before D Day. He returned to his base, walking with a pronounced limp, and said he had been passed fit. Then a message came from the hospital saying that Lieut. Dixon had discharged himself because he was anxious to be back with his flotilla in time for the big events to come.

Dixon, quiet and cool-headed, led his flotilla in a number of successful actions.

Another well-known Coastal Forces leader, Lieut.-Commander Don Bradford, R.N.R., revelled in the opportunities offered around the big anchorage in the bay of the Seine. He, and others like Lieut.-Commander D. McCowan, Lieut.-Commander "Tony" Law, Lieut. Mark Arnold-Forster, Lieut. David Shaw, Lieut. Rodney Sykes, Lieut. Philip Lee, Lieut. Guy Hudson, and Lieut. J. A. (Jumper) Collins (who was killed on the bridge of his boat), knew all the answers and gave the Germans little rope.

Sometimes, however, they had to fight against heavy odds—eight to two was not unusual—but still it was the Germans who ran in the end. There were battles to be fought every night and the M.T.B. men knew that it was vital that the enemy should be prevented from getting through to our shipping.

It was a contest in which brains played a big part. The long experience of such comparatively young officers as Lieut.-Christopher Dreyer, R.N., and Lieut.-Commander Peter Scott, R.N.V.R., enabled them to anticipate many of the German moves. In addition, we introduced certain novel methods which undoubtedly mystified the enemy for some considerable time. Our forces had the benefit of the leadership of Captain P. V. McLaughlin, R.N.

It only remains to be said that, long before the fall of Le Havre, the Germans had found the pace too hot for them and the threat of the E and R-boats had been largely broken. The little ship men had gained their finest victory.

X

ANGLO-AMERICAN SQUADRON

We hold these truths to be self-evident, that all men are created equal ; that they are endowed by their Creator with certain unalienable rights ; that among these are life, liberty, and the pursuit of happiness. That, to secure these rights, governments are instituted among men.

DECLARATION OF INDEPENDENCE.

X

ANGLO-AMERICAN SQUADRON

As the Americans closed in on Cherbourg and the tip of the Cotentin peninsula less than three weeks after D Day, the question arose, " Could sea power help the Army in its final assault on a great port ? "

Some of the most powerful batteries along the Channel were known to be in the forts on the breakwater and around the dock area in Cherbourg. Although it would be difficult to move these guns from their fixed emplacements facing the sea, it was always possible that the Germans might get them into action against the advancing troops.

The batteries had been heavily attacked from the air, but the massive concrete protection given to the guns by the enemy had withstood all but the direct hit.

If it was decided that the Allied naval forces should bombard the Cherbourg forts, there was every chance that a number of the batteries would be silenced. Added to the accuracy of naval gunnery, there were bound to be open casements in the seaward side of the fortifications which would provide an Achilles Heel not offered to the aerial bombers.

On the other hand, to carry out such a bombardment big ships must be risked, and there was no point in risking them if the Army felt they could do without their help.

Before any decision had been reached on the matter I was in Portsmouth, living in the comfortable atmosphere of H.M.S. *Vernon*, the famous torpedo establishment. Among one or two other naval correspondents to have cabins in the *Vernon* was my friend Desmond Tighe, of Reuters.

To us, late one night, came an instruction to be ready to leave at 4.30 the next morning. " It's the bombardment," we said, but we both knew from experience that many things might change whatever plans were afoot, and the best policy was to " wait and see."

In the first light of dawn we left Portsmouth and motored to Portland. Three photographers had joined the party and we shared a car which was driven in the most expert manner by a Wren. (I heard later that she drove her own powerful sports car in peace-time.)

It was a fine morning and a beautiful drive. Although the journey was not a long one, it provided an excellent panorama of the English countryside. First there were glimpses of the Solent and the boat-building yards, with long, flat-bottomed craft to remind one of their direct contribution to the Invasion fleet.

After war-torn Southampton came the dark-green shade of the New Forest, with Lyndhurst slipping by like an island. Then the broader sweeps of Dorset, with the rising sun sharpening the curves of the Downs and creating fantastically long, stabbing fingers of shadow.

Then the first glimpse of Weymouth and its glorious bay, with Portland, a grimly solid sentinel reaching out to sea in the west.

We drove along by the Chesil Beach, past long lines of American heavy tanks, and arrived in Portland before 8 A.M. A one-way traffic arrangement led our driver astray, and the car climbed steadily until we were on the top of the headland and on the road to the Bill.

Retracing our course, we dropped down into the town again, to be greeted by cheerful American coloured troops going off, mess-tins in hand, to breakfast.

Breakfast was a happy thought to us, too, but, after the urgent over-night call and early start, we hardly expected to get any until we were in the ship or ships we had been sent to join. When we reported, however, we were told to proceed to the wardroom and have breakfast in our own time as the ships we were to go to had not yet arrived in port !

The ships, we learned, were the cruisers *Glasgow* and *Enterprise*, and even while we made an excellent meal in the wardroom, we saw them enter the harbour and drop anchor among the other ships lying in the shelter of the breakwater.

It was a case of " so near and yet so far," because our next move was back to another port to report to the U.S. Navy Press Officer. On the way our expert driver got " whistled-up " by a U.S. Army traffic " cop."

Standing at the road junction, he blew a shrill and continuous blast as we swung sharply round the corner. The Wren driver stopped promptly and the Army " cop.", a little man, approached with all the dignity of a London policeman. He delivered himself thus : " Lady, I don't know whether you value your life or not, but I would ask you to have consideration for others. Firstly, there are your own passengers. Now, I guess they value their lives. It's my duty (' dooty ') to protect the lives of all people using that crossing. Very often ambulances pass this way and the sick deserve special consideration. So, secondly, I would ask you to have consideration for me. Now, lady, the way you drove round that corner was dangerous, and I must ask that in future you pay proper attention to my signals and assist me in the execution of my duty."

The whole little homily was delivered with breath-taking politeness which gave no opening for any of the dozen snappy answers our Wren was capable of. The " cop " returned to his post triumphantly.

We found the U.S. Navy Press Officer endeavouring to get some semblance of American office efficiency into the bleak shell of a room placed at his disposal. It can be said of him and practically all the Americans I met at this time that there were no complaints. Any hardship or lack of proper facilities they accepted most cheerfully and set about overcoming them as their small contribution to the general effort of the moment.

It was not easy, apparently, to arrange boat transport in the harbour, so we were invited to lunch at an American Army mess. This gave us the opportunity to spend an hour or two in the port.

Now, however, the town had a strong American

atmosphere. This was emphasised when we lunched at the U.S. Army mess. Such pleasant things as corn-off-the-cob were served by American coloured messmen wearing spotless white jackets, and large cups of creamy American coffee were put on the table with the main course.

During the afternoon we mustered our kit again, collected Press despatch bags, and returned to Portland in order to embark in the British cruisers. Desmond Tighe went to the *Glasgow* and I, with the photographers, went aboard the *Enterprise*.

Although they are in no way sister ships, the *Glasgow* and *Enterprise* have been called the " good companion " ships. This name was given to them after their brilliantly successful action in the Bay of Biscay at the end of 1943.

Contacting a powerful force of enemy destroyers, the two British cruisers engaged them, and in a running fight sank three out of eleven Narvik and Elbing-class vessels. It was a remarkable performance because some of the German ships had guns nearly as large as those of the British cruisers. Naval officers, speaking about the action since, have said to me, " It ought to have been a paradise for the destroyer commanders. What would we not give to have such a force out and be lucky enough to catch two German cruisers."

The *Glasgow* and *Enterprise* became the " good companions " because when the reports went in and attempts were made to access the amount of success achieved by each ship, it was found that neither had made an individual claim. They preferred that the credit should be shared equally by the team.

There is a considerable difference in age between the two ships, the *Glasgow*, a modern " town "-class cruiser, being completed less than two years before the war started. The *Enterprise*, on the other hand, is " getting on." She was ordered during the last war and was completed in 1926. She has a sister ship, the only other one of the same class, H.M.S. *Emerald*.

They are easy to distinguish because, apart from having

the long, low lines of the last war cruisers, they have three funnels unevenly set. Two are close to the bridge and the other is much farther astern.

As I stepped on board the *Enterprise* I felt there was something very British about her, and the thought flashed through my mind that this very ship and this very quarter-deck had represented Britain in many parts of the world. An old ship has an atmosphere and perhaps the quarter-deck for a moment was haunted by all those immaculately uniformed figures who had come aboard in many ports in peace-time, saluting, just as I did, as they set foot on the well-scrubbed woodwork.

No ship in war can be quite as spic and span as in peace-time. There are too many comings and goings, too much sea-time and too little time on the turn round. Stores and ammunition have to be loaded-in just when the Commander would like to see everything on deck trim and tidy.

But there is compensation for this in the feeling that there is real purpose behind all that is going on. Real shells may be heavier than the imaginary, airy things gunners pretended to pass up to the guns in practices before the war, but I have never met a gunner yet who complained about the real thing.

Shells were being passed into the *Enterprise* as we arrived, but the ammunition disappeared down the hatches to the magazines as a pure routine. The only time that one worries about ammunition in the Navy in war-time is when it is running short.

Another thing about H.M. ships in war-time is that they are usually much more short of space than in peace-time. As soon as war is declared, ships' companies are brought up to war strength. That at once swallows up some of the space. Then it is necessary to carry bulks of timber for shoring up damaged parts of the ship in an emergency. Fire-fighting equipment and necessary spare parts and replacements must be stowed with an eye to emergency needs rather than the comfort of officers and crew.

It is not easy, therefore, to accommodate visitors, and it was understandable that the commander and first lieutenant should go into conference, after they had welcomed us, on the subject of where we should sleep. We were quite happy to " shake-down " anywhere and welcomed a suggestion, put forward rather apologetically, that we should sleep in camp-beds on a deck space outside the captain's sea-cabin, at least until the ship went to sea. This had been improved on, however, long before it was time to turn in.

Although we had come at break-neck speed to join the ships, it appeared that there was no hurry. In fact they did not sail until three days later, and by that time one of our party had given up hope of witnessing the bombardment and gone ashore.

There was much of interest to be seen both in the ship and in the harbour during the time we waited. Captain H. Grant, of the Royal Canadian Navy, was in command of the *Enterprise*, and his ship was undoubtedly a happy one. If there was " something on " everyone was quietly confident that the Captain would see that the *Enterprise* played her part in it efficiently and well.

It was a little strange to be in a British ship and to know that the force she would operate with would not be commanded by a British Admiral.

Looking around the harbour one saw that by far the most powerful ships there were those flying the Stars and Stripes. Nothing could have been more encouraging than to realise that, with our own Navy growing daily in power, the United States had moved so far and so fast from the days of Pearl Harbour that, despite her vast commitments in the Pacific, she could send such great warships as the *Nevada, Texas, Arkansas, Tuscaloosa, Augusta* and *Quincy* to fight alongside the Royal Navy in our home waters.

Under Rear-Admiral Alan Kirk, in command of the whole western area sea forces for the invasion, Rear-Admiral Morton L. Deyo, flying his flag in the *Tuscaloosa,* commanded the bombardment unit of which the *Glasgow* and *Enterprise* formed a part.

In their distinctive camouflage of two shades of grey-blue, the American warships lay in Portland while the majority of the boats, passing backwards and forwards to the shore, carried the white-hatted sailors of our Ally.

The Americans certainly predominated in the port, and this was most strongly brought home to me one evening when I was returning to the ship after being ashore. The jetty control was all-American and the majority of sailors arriving to return to their ships were also American. A party of Canadians, with a drawl in their speech, engaged in easy exchanges with the " Yanks," and a west-country " burr " sounded almost out of place. But most American of all was the Chief Petty Officer handling the arrival and departure of boats. With a megaphone to help him, he called the names of the ships as the boats came alongside : " *Tuscaloooosa*," " *R-kan-sa*," " *Ennerprise*," he boomed, while the men scrambled aboard.

One day Desmond Tighe and I " rendezvoused " in a ship from another of our Allies, the Netherlands *Queen Emma*. In a delightfully modern vessel, converted for the uses of war, we enjoyed, for a short time, surroundings more reminiscent of the first stage of a continental holiday than of war. The only two Dutch officers we met on board had become so English in appearance and speech that it was some time before I knew their true nationality.

There was one particularly cheerful evening in the *Enterprise* when a number of American naval officers were entertained. All U.S. warships are " dry," and there is no doubt that the average American officer appreciates the liquid supplies that are to hand in the ward-room of any of H.M. ships. That, however, is incidental to the good comradeship existing between the two services and our own officers will gladly forego their usual evening drink when an invitation comes from an American ship.

Like most ward-rooms, that of the *Enterprise* had its

" characters." In this case it was the Engineer Commander and a young Australian officer, known to all as " Digger." When " Digger " and " the Chief " were determined on a party nobody could stand in the way —or even aside.

Aided by " the Pay " and " the Padre " in particular, they made the evening bright with music. They would both be the first to admit that they needed some assistance because the Engineer Commander, with a true ear for music, was so limited in voice that only those " in the know " could be sure what tunes he was attempting to hum, while " Digger " could produce such volume, with a very limited ear for music, as to make the result the same. Fortunate in the possession of a piano, a gramophone and a comprehensive collection of records, the ward-room of H.M.S. *Enterprise* could soon become the scene of a very jolly party.

The Engineer Commander eventually brought the house down by appearing as a W. W. Jacobs' character in an old blue sweater, a greasy cap and with chin darkened to the shade of a three-days' old growth of beard. He then recited—but what he recited is neither here nor there.

A conference aboard the *Tuscaloosa* on June 24th which was attended by Captain Grant, made everybody expectant. That evening we knew that we were not to be disappointed in our expectations.

The situation around Cherbourg had been developing rapidly, and we knew that the Americans had entered the outskirts of the town and that the Germans only held the thinnest of strips along the top of the peninsula. Would we be allowed to bombard with the American troops so close to the sea, was the question.

When we sailed at dawn on the 25th the impression was that the bombardment was not all-important. The big ships were going to cover the little minesweepers whose task it was to clear a channel to within a few miles of the French port. They would be well within range of the big coastal batteries still in German hands.

The sun rose into a cloudless sky as the *Tuscaloosa* led the combined British and American squadron across the Channel. The big guns of our force were in the U.S. battleship *Nevada*. The other ships with Rear-Admiral Moon were the *Quincy*, a lovely new cruiser with fine lines and sharp bows as beautifully proportioned as those of a yacht, the *Glasgow*, not quite so elegant, but extremely workmanlike and looking particularly powerful from the bridge forward, and the *Enterprise*, prepared to show that a good " old 'un " could keep company with the best of the youngsters.

Two other powerful United States ships, the *Texas* and *Arkansas*, had been detached and formed a strong supporting unit under Rear-Admiral Bryant.

The big ships were swept across the Channel by the Fleet sweepers and other vessels who were to do their main work under the noses of the enemy shore batteries. Out in front were the two smallest vessels of all—two motor launches, making a double sweep to offer protection to the first of the Fleet sweepers. They, too, had work to do on the other side. They would lay the smoke screens between the land and the Allied ships if it became necessary to give them cover.

The channel that we followed was marked at regular intervals with buoys, which meant that some other handmaidens of the Fleet, the Dan buoy-layers, were in attendance.

As the ships steamed steadily along, final preparations were made by the gunners. All guns were closed up and a watchful eye was kept for enemy aircraft. Times had indeed changed from the days when British cruisers, escorting vital convoys through the Mediterranean or to the far north, knew that it was inevitable that there would be long hours of hard fighting with squadron after squadron of Hun aircraft. All the planes we saw on this day, and the total must have run into three figures, were our own.

In the *Enterprise* there was no excitement, but everyone, from the Captain downwards, went about his duties

with a purposefulness which implied that nothing would
be left undone by them which could in any way affect
the ship or their shipmates in the moment of action
Even Mickey, known as " the Damage Control cat '
because he invariably found his way to the Damage
Control centre when the ship was in action, appeared
to be ready to move off to his action station at the sound
of the first gun.

The crew wore their light cotton hoods and gloves
which offer protection against the flash of the guns
With the gloves pulled well up their arms and steel
helmets worn on top of the hoods, they took on a new
uniformity, suggestive of machine-like efficiency. Some
had tucked their trousers into the tops of their socks
as an added guard against the searing flames which
belch out of the guns in a heavy cloud of yellow cordite
smoke.

Whatever their appearance, the men themselves were
anything but automatons. Here and there a quip would
raise a roar of laughter. Sometimes a man would swear
The majority were content to work quietly on whatever
piece of mechanism they were responsible for or, if there
was nothing more to be done, to sit in an odd corner
and enjoy the warmth of the sun. One, I noticed, was
sitting on the deck, with his back propped against a
stanchion, absorbed in a book. The title of the book
was " Mutiny on the *Bounty*."

Occasionally the question was raised, " When's the
char (the sailor's word for tea) coming up ? " It re
minded one that in a ship the immediate approach to
battle may be made in curious places—the galley, the
sick bay or even the ship's office.

When we were still fifteen miles from the French coast
a curious thing happened. The horizon ahead of us lost
its sharpness as though a mist had risen. At first it was
taken for mist caused by the heat and coming from the land
In a short time, however, there came a strong smell of
burning and it was realised that the smudged horizon
was due to a great belt of thin smoke blowing out to sea

from the terrific fires raging along the battle front around Cherbourg.

The smoke was thick enough to hide the coast at a distance and there was no point in straining one's eyes. It was to our ears that the first real indication came that we were rapidly closing the land. A low thunder which could be heard above the noises of the ship and the slight swish of the water, and which was added to occasionally by larger and more distinct "thumps," gradually became evident. It was the noise of battle on the mainland and the "thumps" were heavy bombs going down from our aircraft on to the German-held fortifications.

The distant rumble acted like a tonic in the *Enterprise*, putting everybody on his toes. Previously one would have said that the ship was ready for instant action, but the actual sound of the guns provided just that little extra something which makes an international football match or a championship fight a matter of special importance.

"Aircraft bearing Red 10," reported the lookout, his binoculars still raised skywards. For a moment we wondered if the Luftwaffe would make a last-minute attempt to turn us from our destination. It was odd to think that not so many months earlier it would have been regarded as next to suicidal to put big ships close in to the French shore.

Looking up at the aircraft, identified as our own Lightnings, there came the realisation that we had never really expected them to be enemy planes. Fluctuations which are not possible in sea-power are easily accepted in regard to air-power. Even the gunners, who in the early days of the war had every reason to expect practically all aircraft to be hostile, had come to accept the idea that the R.A.F. and U.S. Air Forces were completely on top in the air. Even so, they remained as alert as ever at their guns.

When we were about twelve miles off the French coast, four British destroyers came up from the eastward.

They were probably the patrol covering the anchorages off the American beaches on the eastern side of the Cotentin.

The British ships swung across our stern, just as Rear-Admiral Deyo's force turned on to an easterly course. They passed close to the U.S. destroyers which had screened the big ships across the Channel.

None of these evolutions disturbed the sweepers in the slightest. They, too, had turned but they kept on sweeping at the same steady speed, and continued to do so all through the exciting hours that followed.

For a short time the *Nevada* and the British and American cruisers, their big battle ensigns standing out magnificently in the strong sunlight, continued on a course which took them parallel with the French coast at a distance of about nine miles. It was possible to see the land, although the smoke-haze was deceptive enough to make it still seem a very long way off.

On the bridge of the *Enterprise*, Captain Grant and other officers were studying the blurred coastline intently. Occasionally they lowered their binoculars in order to draw attention to a particular feature that had been identified. Captain Grant, wearing a deep American-type " tin hat "—the only one in the ship, as far as I could see—sat comfortably on top of a chart cabinet.

An officer found time to point out to me our position on a large scale chart. " We are well within range of the 11 in. guns in the shore batteries," he said. " We shall be turning presently to go in on the last leg," he added. " When we are about five to six miles off Cherbourg we shall turn and run on a parallel course again, while the minesweepers finish their task. If the Germans do not open fire on the minesweepers, or us, I doubt if there will be any battle, because our first aim is to cover the sweepers while they finish their job."

A fair impression of what was to take place had been given to the ship's company earlier in the morning, when Captain Grant made a short and to-the-point broadcast over the loud-speaker system. It had given considerable

satisfaction because the sailors felt that they were going
to be of direct assistance to the American soldiers fighting
so well ashore.

While I was still on the bridge, an officer said, " The
minesweepers have turned on to their new course for the
final run in towards Cherbourg," and, with a thrill, I
realised that the moment had come when a direct challenge
would be delivered by the Anglo-American naval force to
the Germans in the Cherbourg fortresses.

The sweepers—at least one little trawler was amongst
them—went in under the enemy guns with a nonchalant
air of " do not bother us, we have some work to do."
The even smaller M.L.'s went with them, still dutifully
sweeping for the sweepers, and the big ships followed
after.

No sight could have been more stirring. From the
J. 65, the J. 27, the J. 00, the T. 350 and many other
little vessels, there fluttered battle ensigns almost as big
as those flown from the cruisers. No ships, I felt, were
more entitled to them. And in company with the White
Ensign there went the Stars and Stripes. The two flags
which symbolise the freedom of the seas were to wave
together in battle.

" That's one of the *Dance* class," said a sailor, following
my gaze in the direction of the sweepers. The name
fitted exactly.

As we took up our new station astern of the *Glasgow*,
speed was increased. The French coast stood out much
more clearly and there was no doubt that the enemy
could see us and probably already had his guns trained
upon us.

A little earlier, I had gone down inside the ship through
the tiny emergency hatches which are the only entrances
and exits available during action. Many of the crew
were lying around between decks looking fairly comfortable and certainly warm in their flash-proof kit. They
were obeying an order that, in action, all personnel are to
lie down when not actively engaged at work.

I thought of all these men below decks in the *Enterprise*

as we closed with the enemy.   Many of them would be too preoccupied in their tasks to worry about events outside the ship.   Others would have plenty of time to think and imagine.   They would hear and feel our own guns, know if the ship was turning sharply or going at speed, and would not be left unaware if the enemy shells fell too close.

The best commentary on the attitude of these men who go, as it were, blindly into battle came after the bombardment from the Engineer Commander.   " There was a new boy down with me," he said.   " I was lying down reading the paper.   There's not much for me to do—they do it all.   The new boy was lying flat on his back and looked damned uncomfortable.   I told him to go and get himself a pillow. . . ."

The atmosphere above decks was electric, because at any moment the signal might be given for a duel between heavy calibre guns ashore and afloat.

The signal came after the little ships had turned on to their final sweeping area, less than five miles from the outer breakwater of Cherbourg harbour.   It came from a German battery which opened fire on the mine-sweepers.

At once the big ships replied.   One of the first salvoes roared out of the *Enterprise's* forward turret, the flame from the guns sending a gust of warm air back over the signal-bridge.   Fore and aft, great bursts of flame from the *Glasgow* and the American cruisers were followed by the thunder of the guns.

Thus challenged, the Germans promptly transferred their fire to the fighting ships.   Their first shells, splashing in the water, made it clear that they had a very good idea of the range.   The 14-inch guns of the *Nevada* sent huge projectiles screaming back towards the shore.   More shells from the enemy burst around the bombarding vessels and the M.L.'s raced in to lay a smoke screen between the ships and the shore.   Shells from both sides went high over them as they did so.

Also between the ships and the shore were some of the

minesweepers, still imperturbably going about their business.

Before the bombardment started 1 had heard that Admiral Deyo was prepared to shell the enemy positions for ninety minutes. This time had been agreed to apparently by the military commanders on shore, where the position was changing so rapidly that it was impossible to guarantee how far forward our own troops would be in a matter of hours.

Almost unconsciously one looked at the clock when the first guns roared and marked the time when all the noise, excitement and danger would end. Three hours later the guns of the Anglo-American naval force were still thundering although the fire from the shore batteries had slackened appreciably.

During those three hours the Germans suffered one of the most severe batterings of the war from naval armaments. In the early stages of the bombardment the pace was very hot indeed. All the ships were firing constantly and many shells fell on to the five miles stretch of swept waters which formed their gun platform.

The ships were acting independently and moving at speed and zig-zagging to upset the predicted fire of the enemy. Up and down they went, passing one another first to port and then to starboard, as if engaged in some great counter-march like the massed bands of pre-war Aldershot tattoos. The *Enterprise*, turning at speed, heeled over as if she were no more than a big destroyer instead of a seven thousand odd tons ship.

The *Nevada* and the American cruisers were getting off an impressive number of rounds and the *Glasgow* was particularly belligerent. Occasionally she appeared almost to stop in order to slash shells back more accurately at a troublesome battery on the shore. On several occasions she was straddled, great fountains of water going up to the left and right of her.

She was hit by a shell in one of the hangars just abaft the bridge and a fire was started. When this was reported to the Admiral he ordered her out of action, but she reported fit for duty again in a quarter of an hour and returned to the thick of it. She continued to fire with all guns until the bombardment ended.

A number of German shells fell uncomfortably close to the *Enterprise* but as men went about their duties they were smiling and there was a light in their eyes such as other British sailors must have had in many other ships through the years of fighting that gave us our unbeatable naval tradition.

If they worried at all, they worried about their good companion ship, the *Glasgow*. "They are dead-set on the old *Glasgow* but she's giving it to 'em back with interest," I heard one rating saying, and his eyes were fixed on the other British cruiser, although the blast of our own guns hit one in the face like a scorching wind. A cigarette I was smoking was whipped out of my mouth as cleanly as if it had been snatched by hand.

As time went on men came along with ugly bits of shell splinter which they displayed with pride. "Fell just beside me," "Picked it up on the flag deck," they said, and passed on.

Then word went round that the Commander, Commander J. W. Hoskins, R.N., had been struck by one of these splinters while at his action station in the after part of the ship. Because it is the Commander's task in a ship to organise and supervise most of the every-day work, he can seldom expect to be the most popular man on board. But when that ragged German shell splinter tore into the shoulder of the Commander of the *Enterprise*, painful as it was, it made him both popular and important. The men of the *Enterprise* felt that the Germans had gone out of their way to strike at a not too young senior officer of *their* ship. "The so-and-so's!" they said, and a fresh wave of energy swept through the ship.

A little later there came another disturbing rumour on the ship's bush telegraphy. "The Captain has been wounded on the bridge," it said. It was not easy to obtain confirmation or denial because it was known that

the Captain was still at his post. The feeling this time
was one of complete indignation.

The rumour was true, but although I went to the
bridge and talked with the Captain, it was not until an
hour later that I knew that the wound was quite a nasty
one.

I found him passing orders without a trace of excitement. He was moving about normally and when I told
him of the rumour he said, " Oh, something bounced on
to my shoulder and knocked me over. It feels a bit
bruised."

He then told me that from spotter aircraft we had had
reports of the success of the shooting. " They tell us
that seventy-five per cent. of our fire is effective," he
said. " We have certainly silenced a number of the
batteries, although we cannot be certain at the moment
that we have knocked them out."

Later, when the bombardment had ended I was in the
Captain's cabin, which had been turned into an emergency operating theatre, and saw his tunic brought in by
his steward. The sleeve was pulled inside out and was
soaked with blood. Although he had received an injec-
tion, Captain Grant was still on the bridge and remained
there until his ship was safely back in British waters.

The magnificent courage he displayed was not only
worthy of our own best traditions but should write a
splendid page in the wartime history of the Royal
Canadian Navy.

I would like here, too, to pay tribute to the three
photographers, Lieut. Allen, of the Admiralty Press
Division, Mr. Greenwood, of the *Times* newspaper, and
Mr. Turner, a cinematograph representative, who throughout the bombardment remained on an exposed upper
deck in order to get a pictorial record of the occasion.
To them, as to other news photographers, it was all in
the day's work, but that does not detract from a plucky
performance.

And as we steamed away from the area, men were told-
off from the gun crews, the bridge, the engine-room, the

control centre, the sick bay, in fact, from every part of the ship, to go and collect the rations. They came back happily with big trays of meat sandwiches, cut to anything but dainty proportions, and cans full of hot soup. Down in the galley I found the cooks who had prepared no less than fifteen hundred sandwiches and who were perspiring quite as freely as the actual fighting personnel as they ladled out the steaming soup.

Before the Allied ships reached England they received a signal from Admiral Deyo in which he thanked all officers and men for their fine performance against efficient enemy batteries, which had been of the greatest value to the army at a most opportune moment.

His own contribution had been to see that the Germans were shelled for exactly twice as long as had originally been intended.

XI

GATEWAY TO THE CONTINENT

*Shall we not sail against his territory?
" Where shall we find a landing-place? "
someone asks. The war itself will discover
the weak places in his position.*

DEMOSTHENES.

H.M.S. "GLASGOW" BOMBARDING, WITH THE U.S.S. "QUINCY" STEAMING ON A PARALLEL COURSE

XI

GATEWAY TO THE CONTINENT

CHERBOURG fell to the Americans very shortly after the naval bombardment, and immediately became a Mecca for War Correspondents.

Some, indeed, had entered the City while fighting was still in progress. Among them was Richard MacMillan, well-known correspondent of the British United Press, with whom I crossed from Southampton to Cherbourg in the first party of war correspondents to leave England—in October, 1939.

Although continuously in the field from that time, MacMillan ran into real trouble for the first time when he was wounded by a shell splinter in the outskirts of Cherbourg. Fortunately the wound was not serious and " Mac," as he is known to all his friends, carried on and got through one more typically vivid, straightforward despatch.

My approach to Cherbourg, however, had to be made by sea and I knew there was little chance of entering the port overnight. Like the mills of God, the Navy grinds exceeding small, but seldom hurries the process.

Among the public there was a rather thoughtless wave of optimism when the news of the capitulation of Cherbourg first came through. " Now," they said, " We have one of the finest ports in France. The biggest liners used to call there regularly before the war. From to-day there is no limit to the amount of man power and war material we can pour into France."

There seemed to be a vague idea that the *Queen Elizabeth* and *Queen Mary*, aided by a few other giant liners, would proceed to shuttle countless men and guns in straight runs between New York and Cherbourg and Southampton and Cherbourg.

This was the German nightmare, too, and they had

been in control of the French port for a long time. If one stopped to think about it for only a few minutes one realised that the Germans would have done everything in their power to bar the Allies from having the free use of Cherbourg as a port, even after its capture.

Both the United States and British naval experts were well prepared for what we eventually found in Cherbourg. Ashore there were the very extensive demolitions, particularly in the important naval area, and in the harbour there were the mines.

For more than a week after the fall of Cherbourg I waited in Portsmouth for the opportunity to join a ship crossing to the French port.

Day by day, burly, cheerful Commander Dillon Robinson, Chief R.N. Press Liaison officer, shook his head and, with a quizzical look in his eye, said, " As before," which meant that there was no passage to Normandy that day for me.

Reports filtered back of extensive damage to dock and other waterside installations and a fantastic amount of mining in Cherbourg's wonderful harbour.

Whether these were true or not, it was evident that the naval authorities were making a thorough examination of the situation. One might reverse the old adage and say that the angels were doing a lot of delicate stepping before any fools had a chance to rush in.

If Cherbourg had been vital as a point of intake to General Montgomery's Allied Armies, I have no doubt that big cargoes would have been unloaded inside the magnificent outer breakwater within forty-eight hours of the capture of the port. But the beach supply system had worked so splendidly all along our section of coast that we could afford to take the necessary time to deal systematically with Cherbourg.

Neither was it time wasted, because the early entry of ships into the harbour would inevitably have meant a proportion of losses. These losses, which might have been fairly heavy, would not have been as serious as the lasting dislocation caused by sunken ships in the harbour.

So Rear-Admiral Boyd, of the United States Navy, commanding the western area off the Normandy coast, with Commodore Sullivan, U.S.N., and other British and American specialist officers, made full and careful inspection and then decided on their final plans for countering the worst the Germans had been able to do.

On the evening of July 12th I suddenly received instructions to go aboard H.M.S. *Franklin* that night.

With Stanley Maxted of the B.B.C. I went out in a despatch boat to find the *Franklin*, which was lying somewhere off the Isle of Wight. It was a cold and blustery evening, much more like October than July, but Maxted, a typically tough Canadian, had no coat to go over his battle-dress—he had had no time to collect one. He wore the medal ribbons of the last war, carried himself like a soldier, and by no stretch of the imagination could be said to have what is sometimes called " the B.B.C. manner."

We were most hospitably received in the *Franklin*, a ship of 800 tons of the Fleet minesweeper type. She and her sister ship, the *Scott*, are Royal Navy survey vessels and are specially fitted for this important work.

In command of the *Franklin* was Commander E. G. Irving, R.N., one of the Navy's survey experts. Most of the officers and men had been trained in this branch, which gives to the Navy much of its immense knowledge of inshore waters all over the world. H.M.S. *Franklin* does not carry a navigator because, in effect, all her officers are, incidentally, as it were, trained navigators.

Early the next morning we sailed for Cherbourg in the company of a new Canadian corvette. The journey to France was uneventful except for one " contact " while we were still in sight of the English coast. Taking no chances, we circled over it for a time and dropped depth-charges. After each shattering explosion, the crew clustered around the rails eagerly looking for any sign of wreckage. One rating arrived in a hurry with a sort of Father Neptune trident on a long pole. Believing that " it is an ill-wind that blows nobody any good," he was ready to spear any fish that might be rocketed to the surface by the under-water explosions.

Actually all that happened after each big " bang " was the appearance of a long-faced rating from below carrying a couple of broken cups, plates or tumblers, which followed the course taken a few minutes earlier by the depth-charge.

Towards midday we sighted the French coast and presently picked out Cherbourg with its long protecting breakwater. About the same time a search of the western horizon through powerful binoculars revealed other land—the island of Alderney, still in German hands. It was curious to think that the enemy, with every reason for anxiety as to their own position, had probably spotted us as quickly as we spotted them.

Another thought that came to me was that not many days earlier I had approached exactly the same headland and had met a very different reception. As we closed in I picked out the low, menacing shapes of the forts on the breakwater which, on the previous occasion, were manned by Nazis trying desperately to destroy the British and American warships attacking them. One instinctively kept a wary eye on the battlements.

One big fort on the eastern end of the centre section of the breakwater had been smashed into a mass of rubble, and it was very satisfying to learn later that naval guns were responsible for this.

A group of British minesweepers, B.Y.M.S.'s, were sweeping outside the breakwater as we entered the harbour. Inside, smaller M.L.'s had their big red sweeping flags flying as they moved in pairs over these dangerous waters.

One fair-sized American ship was already at anchor in the outer harbour and the *Franklin* moved slowly in her direction. It was a tense moment because no ship of our size had crossed the harbour since the departure of the Germans. Constant sweeps had been carried out for several days, but it was known that the Hun had used various types of mine and the question was, " Would we set off something that had evaded the sweeps ? "

It was therefore with a sense of relief that one heard the Captain's order to drop anchor.

The " hook " went down with a rattle and a roar as the heavy chain ran out into deep water and the *Franklin* swung easily, about two hundred yards from one of the big forts on the breakwater. It was interesting to note that this, and other forts in the vicinity, had been badly smashed about on the landward side. There had been some very accurate shelling by the U.S. Army gunners.

The long mole protecting the inner harbour had a big gap torn in its high wall which was clearly an enemy demolition effort. The stout stone base was little more than dented and lorries were busy tipping their loads in order that the surface should be quickly restored.

Almost before the survey ship was at anchor, an R.N. lieutenant-commander came on board. One of the first to move into Cherbourg after its capture, he had been engaged in directing part of the harbour clearance organisation and was able to give Commander Irving a brief but comprehensive picture of the general situation.

As he talked he ate a plate of cold meat and salad— the mustard and cress being grown on board by the Captain's steward—which he described as his first " civilised meal for a fortnight." He thoughtfully left behind a small tin of meat and a packet of biscuits, his U.S. Army ration, about which he had no complaints beyond the fact that fourteen days of exactly similar food makes it rather monotonous.

Little more than an hour after the *Franklin's* arrival her boats were away on their first surveying task, the location of wrecks in the harbour.

As the boats headed away from the ship, the B.Y.M.S., doing a magnetic sweep in the inner harbour, set off a big mine which sent a mighty cascade of water into the air just round the corner of the mole.

The commanding officers of some M.L.'s which came alongside the Survey ship just afterwards, mentioned that they had been over the position of the explosion many times while doing non-magnetic sweeps.

From these young R.N.V.R. officers, whose small vessels had been right in the van of the Allied approach by sea to Cherbourg, I heard a thrilling story.

Although they had been sweeping for ten days, whenever the state of the tide permitted, they showed few signs of the long strain imposed by such duties, beyond a very natural physical tiredness. They laughed and joked about odd incidents during their sweeps and could even see the funny side of such mishaps as getting a mine caught up in a sweep and having to tow it out to sea.

While drinking water was pumped from the *Franklin* into the empty tanks of the M.L.'s, I sat in one of the little ward-rooms, and this is what I heard :

" We were sent to sweep the inner harbour and have been at it steadily ever since we started. There were quite a few mines, as we soon discovered. The M.L.'s between them have collected a nice ' bag ' and have suffered no casualties, although there have been a few hair-raising moments."

One of these, I was told, was when a mine suddenly shot to the surface after the sweep had been pulled in close to the boat. A Petty Officer saved the situation because, as soon as he saw what was being pulled in, he grabbed a chopper and in one terrific slash severed the sweep and its lethal attachment.

Lieut. G. D. de Lange, a Londoner, commanded the first M.L. to enter Cherbourg harbour. One of his sweeps produced a strange catch. " We knew we had something odd in the sweep," he said, " and therefore treated it with particular respect. When it broke water we found we had dragged up half a Heinkel ! "

Another young bearded Commanding Officer, Sub-Lieut. J. B. F. Foxlee, told of two grateful Americans who were picked up after their boat had overturned. " Next day they sent us a huge hamper of comforts— the largest an M.L. has ever received, I should think," he said.

One flat-bottomed craft, smaller than any of the M.L.'s, had met with disaster when she ran right on to a mine. Two of her crew had miraculous escapes, one swimming 150 yards with a broken arm and in a semi-conscious condition as a result of concussion.

Lieut. de Lange laughed with the rest when they gave an account of how he had been called to a conference when he was in the midst of clearing an obstruction from one of his propellers. The Commanding Officer himself had gone over the side " in his birthday suit " to work on the obstruction. When the signal for the conference arrived he had to move in a hurry. He just had time to dry himself and then rushed off with a bundle of clothes under his arm, stopping at intervals to slip into a garment.

While the M.L.'s were still alongside the *Franklin* their relief arrived. The incoming boats were received with a rousing cheer. They came alongside, too, and a real little ship party began.

The new-comers looked with interest at the roughly-chalked stripes on the squat funnels of the boats that had been engaged in sweeping. Each stripe, they knew, represented the disposal of a considerable amount of high explosive with which the Germans had hoped to account for a ship, her cargo and perhaps a number of her crew.

The chalk stripes appeared to make them additionally eager to take on the responsible and dangerous task performed so capably by their gallant sister ships.

Much remained for the sweepers to do, odd mines going up all through the following week while I was still in Cherbourg. The harbour has an immense area, and it was clearly beyond the power of the Germans to " cover " it with mines, as first reports had suggested. But the mixture of mines they had put down made it necessary to carry out various types of sweeps over the same area.

The German demolitions in the naval dockyard area, which I saw after my arrival, were almost beyond description. High explosives had been used in vast quantities to bring buildings tumbling down, to break up machines, to sink vessels and to smash and destroy in every direction.

By a strange irony the enemy had found the greatest difficulty in destroying the structures which he himself had built to resist the visitations of Allied bombers.

One end of the concrete roof of the E-boat pens had been lifted solidly and a huge twenty-feet thick slab of concrete, with an area larger than that of a tennis court, perched crazily above ruined walls. The pens themselves, which had been built like vast subterranean caverns to allow for the twenty to thirty-feet rise and fall of tide on this part of the coast, appeared to be undamaged.

Fires had raged in the big stores buildings and it was not difficult to construct in one's mind the inferno that must have existed behind the German soldiers as they were driven back into Cherbourg by the advancing Americans.

At the entrance to the great machine-shop I met a solitary blue-overalled French workman. He stood as though still dazed and mechanically touched his peaked cap in acknowledgment of a greeting. When I spoke to him he could say no more than the one word " Terrible, terrible, terrible . . ." in a voice which still shook.

Hundreds of machines, built for the finest precision work, had been dealt with by the Germans, one by one. Most of them had suffered under charges of high explosives. Here and there, perhaps because the explosive failed, gear-boxes and other vital parts had been smashed in with sledge-hammers.

Most of the roof had been blown off the building, yet a doll, hanging by a bench where a man had worked, still dangled at the end of its string. A number of Belgians, I was told, had been imported by the Germans to work in the yards. Where they had gone to nobody appeared to know.

In the midst of the most devastated area one small building had managed to survive. It was already being put to use and the notice on the door stood out as a symbol. " The French Navy," it said.

In other areas the Americans had set to work with typical thoroughness and already had buildings sufficiently ship-shape to be put into use as offices. Among the ruins the American services had managed to produce more than a touch of what is known in their own country as " big business efficiency."

Portable filing systems, coming in on an early priority, were in use and the khaki-clad office staffs were running their fingers through them as easily and quickly as they would have done if they had been housed in a New York skyscraper.

When the Americans first entered the dock area in Cherbourg it was impossible to drive a vehicle on the roads because of the piles of rubble and broken glass. All this had been cleared aside when I saw it and the roads were open to an endless stream of vehicles, many of them heavy lorries in which coloured troops of the United States Army rode triumphantly off with one more load of débris.

One big seaplane hangar which the Germans had sought to destroy had its roof touching the ground on one side, while the back bulged like a giant concertina. A little shoring up had made it safe, however, and the American engineers were hard at work inside under the cover of what looked like a huge half-collapsed umbrella.

There was every justification for the remark of one officer : " The Allied Air Forces have sent the Germans concrete crazy ! " On all sides there was evidence of the underground life led by the enemy.

Forts, pill-boxes, dug-outs, hideouts all plunged straight into the earth and had the protection of varying thicknesses of concrete. It was not easy to examine them because few had been cleared of the confused mass of bedding and other things left behind by the Germans, and all of them were as dark as the Black Hole of Calcutta, no electricity being available.

Some of them were as big as a tube railway station, with dozens of cubicles built off the main tunnel ; others had room for no more than two persons.

For those who manned the coastal guns there were underground chambers immediately beneath the gun

positions.   They were sub-divided to give added strength
and each concrete-surrounded compartment housed about
a dozen men.   In the middle of the compartment was a
plain wooden table and each man had a small unpainted
wooden cupboard for his personal belongings.

A remarkable amount of bread was to be found in the
majority of these hideouts.   In many cases more than
a dozen mouldy loaves were still on tables and ledges
ten days after the inhabitants had been cleared out.
The German soldiers had also provided themselves with
ample supplies of French mineral waters.   It was natural
to conclude that they have always had at the back of
their minds the need that might arise for the bare
necessities of life in the case of siege.

Their equipment was, on the whole, good.   The belts and
cartridge pouches were made of stout leather and their
metal mess-tins were light and strong.   Much use had been
made of a very light metal for spoons and forks and all small
articles.   It was clearly some composition metal, but
would not bend and was too hard to snap with the hands.

Most prolific of all supplies was ammunition.   It was
present in all forms, from large shells to the dyed wooden
bullets used for close-range fighting.   Hundreds of
thousands of rounds of ammunition must have been
left in the forts and underground shelters.   Occasionally
the Americans took a belt and hung it garland fashion
over the bonnet of a lorry.   It was to be found in practically all strong-points and was far too common to be
treated as a worthwhile souvenir.

German helmets were the most sought-after souvenirs,
but these usually proved too clumsy for their possessors
to retain for long.   They became instead an odd form of
currency.   A good helmet could always be guaranteed
to produce, on exchange, a couple of packets of cigarettes
or a little yellow " Minen " flag.   The latter, triangular
in shape and with a black skull and crossbones depicted
on it, achieved popularity because it could be conveniently carried.

Plenty of first-aid equipment was available for the

Germans who had manned the coastal gun positions, but it was significant that they had provided themselves with French cotton bandages in addition to the *crêpé* paper ones sent out from the Fatherland.

Passing from the melancholy dockyard area with its gaunt skeletons of buildings and broken machinery, one was gratified to find the town of Cherbourg itself almost intact. A few of the larger buildings, such as churches, had been damaged, and infrequently one came upon a gap where an odd shell had fallen short and brought down a house or two.

It was clear from the way these buildings had crumpled up that if the Americans had been indescriminate in their gunnery as they approached the city great damage would have been inflicted on the civilian area. By the time they got through the suburbs, however, the Germans were " on the run " and were cleaned up rapidly, street by street. There were many signs of this grim street fighting. Walls were seared and scared where bullets and light cannon shells had ripped along them and the familiar French window shutters were often splintered and broken. Those who were among the first in Cherbourg after the German capitulation told me that the town itself was like a place of the dead. Slowly the population began to trickle back.

On the walls were still the notices, posted by the Germans, telling them to evacuate the town. There were other notices, too, forbidding all forms of transport in an area extending six kilometres from Cherbourg and posters urging the French inhabitants to go and work in Germany. One, in colour, depicted two strong hands holding a stone in place in a wall, beyond which a great fire burned. Underneath were the words, " Every day spent at work in Germany helps to maintain the security of France." Few of these posters had survived the attentions of the freed French people.

In many places a new poster had appeared. In the background it bore the dark shadow of the swastika ; on top was daubed the bright blue, white and red of France.

Chalked on many walls one saw " Vive la France," " Vive de Gaulle," and " Vive les Alles." There were similiar greetings for Churchill, Roosevelt, Koenig, Stalin, Alexander, Montgomery, Eisenhower, Cunningham and Eden.

July 14th, Bastille Day, was the first occasion after the Allied liberation of Cherbourg that saw the people of the city turn out in strength.

With typical French resilience the younger women appeared looking remarkably chic in their best clothes and really notable hats. More than once American soldiers, used, possibly, to the smart clothes of New York, remarked in wonder at the hats that came on parade in Cherbourg on Bastille Day, 1944. " Gee, ain't that wonderful ! " and " Take a look at that ! " they said, and the French girls, despite their straight faces, were obviously flattered.

Just as interesting were the older people who arrived from outside the town in tumble-down lorries which had known the Normandy roads a long time before the Germans did. Middle-aged and elderly women wore the long black full-skirted dresses and white starched head-wear which most of the young service men from Britain and America could only have seen previously in their school history or geography books.

Often the faces of the women were almost as weather-beaten as those of the men who came with them—old men for the most part, wearing dark suits of strangely venerable cut. It was clear that many of these women had spent long hours working in the fields to make up for the conspicuous absence of young men, most of whom had been taken off to Germany or were among the mass of French prisoners of war still in German hands.

Many of the French flags bore the Cross of Lorraine in their middle panel. Sometimes the red double cross was not quite in the centre of its white background. The emblem of Liberty, which certainly would never have been tolerated by the Germans, had probably been added by old or infirm hands.

A band appeared from somewhere and a long procession was formed. The people marched along with a new pride in their freed city.

One old Frenchman, who turned in his tracks and walked back some distance to direct me to a building I was looking for, spoke with emotion of his feelings. Anxiously and pathetically he asked, " Will liberty come to the whole of France very soon ? "

His concern, I am confident, was felt by the mass of Frenchmen, but there were exceptions. One old farmer said, " To me, and I speak without wishing to give offence, it matters little who is here. I work in the same way and make little more than a living. Before the war and under the Germans it was the same, and it will be the same now." Through such dangerously simple minds the Nazis hoped to consolidate their conquests.

The only purchases permitted to Allied servicemen by the military authorities at this time were green vegetables, which soon appeared in the markets in profusion, and refreshments (but not meals) in the cafés between certain hours.

The vegetables were not expensive ; the refreshments were. The prices charged were the same as were enforced by the Germans, and one could only conclude that the enemy had a good many more francs to play with than our own troops. The exchange rate was fixed for us at 200 francs to the pound. Prices, still to be seen on the same cards as the Germans knew, included twenty francs (two shillings) for a glass of weak French beer, fifteen francs (eighteen pence) for a glass of ordinary red wine and twenty-five francs (two shillings and six-pence) for a small glass of brandy. Before the war the prices would have been roughly twopence for the beer, fourpence for the wine, and sixpence or eightpence for the brandy.

The one meal I had in a restaurant in Cherbourg at this time was cheap. I paid thirty francs, but perhaps the circumstances were exceptional. Passing through one of the narrow side streets, I noticed a little restaurant was one of the few places open. My eye was caught by a tray full of fine rounded leaf artichokes, already cooked. To me they were most tempting, and with no idea of taking any of the more sustaining rations of the local inhabitants, I went in.

The atmosphere was charmingly French. In the little shop Madame prepared the food personally and customers passing through to climb the narrow winding staircase to the dining-room on the first floor could see the good things to come.

As was to be expected, there were no vacant places in the salle-à-manger, but madame would not hear of my leaving her establishment. A place was made for me at the American-cloth-covered family table in the shop. A small bottle of rough cider was placed in front of me and she then proceeded to serve me with a simple and perfectly cooked meal. First there was *pâte* with chopped onion and parsley, then braised tongue, new potatoes and thick brown gravy and finally rich Normandy cream cheese to go with the heavy dark war-time bread.

The artichokes were not on the menu for me, but in the face of such delightful hospitality I could not reveal what had attracted me into the little establishment.

The Frenchman who sat beside me at this meal, and who could not speak a word of English, was happy to show me a permit issued to him by the American authorities which stated in English that he was allowed to go to work in the dock area. He regarded it as the passport of a loyal Frenchman.

Further exploration of Cherbourg revealed the station area as a badly smashed zone. Most of the big station itself—familiar to hundreds of thousands of travellers to Europe from the United States before the war—remained intact, but the blast of demolition explosions nearby had swept through it. There had also been fighting there, as the scarred walls proved.

Some of the huge cranes along the landing stage beside the station had been toppled into the water, while others rested drunkenly against the station itself.

The basin was heavily mined, and for days afterwards giant explosions rocked this part of the town as the mines were disposed of by the intrepid sweepers and disposal experts. Some of the rail trucks left behind by the enemy were German rolling stock and bore the names of such places as Hamburg and Munich.

All through these days and weeks, as Cherbourg slowly returned to life, brave men faced dangers equal to those which must be faced in the front line, in day and night efforts to make safe and restore the port area so that it might serve the Allied Armies.

Among those who led the British units engaged in this work were Commander J. B. G. Temple, D.S.C., R.N., and Commander F. L. De Spon, R.N.R., who were particularly concerned with the clearance of mines, and Commander A. E. Doran, D.S.C., R.N., who was in charge of the harbour sweepings.

With bearded Commander De Spon, I made one brief tour of the outer harbour. It was sufficient to show me the arduous nature of his task. Before I joined him he had collected two snag lines from mines left by the enemy. This entailed picking up buoyed ropes floating almost hidden along the surface of the water, making an attachment to them and then deliberately firing the heavy mines to which they were attached. Following that there was a personal examination of suspicious objects reported by various craft. The whole of this work was carried out in a flimsy, flat-bottomed craft, similar to the one which had been blown to fragments only a few days earlier.

Many types of mine were used by the Germans in their efforts to hold up our use of the port.

The specially equipped boats of H.M.S. *Franklin* were carrying out their meticulous survey of the harbour. At 7.30 each morning the boats left the parent ship and began their up-and-down runs across the harbour waters.

In one of them, commanded by Sub-Lieut. D. P. D. Scott, I spent an interesting forenoon. With a crew of five ratings he covered many carefully checked courses.

All the time an echo-sounding instrument ticked away recordings of the depth of water beneath. A wreck was located and immediately a deep wedge appeared above the level depths marked for the surrounding water. It was necessary to pass many times over the wreck before it could be accurately plotted over its entire length.

In the evening, when the boats returned, all the soundings had to be set down on big charts and frequently the officers of the ship were still poring over the chart-table at midnight. So it was that within a week of H.M.S. *Franklin's* arrival in Cherbourg harbour Commander Irving had forwarded a first-class chart showing actual depths of water for a large part of the outer harbour and some of the inner harbour.

Sometimes it was necessary for a diver to go down and check unusual features on the bed of the sea. This angle of the work fascinated my friend, Stanley Maxted, and before he returned to England he himself went down in full deep-sea diver's equipment and made a broadcast recording from the ocean bed.

The first reward for all these labours came when the big Liberty ships entered the harbour with large-scale supplies for the Allied forces.

Watched by many anxious eyes, four ships came in and moved slowly to their marked anchorages near the outer breakwater. One after the other they dropped anchor and, with a sigh of relief, those who had striven mightily to give these ships safe passage into the first big French port to fall into Allied hands realised that they had not worked in vain.

ADMIRAL SIR BERTRAM RAMSAY, ALLIED NAVAL COMMANDER-IN-CHIEF
FOR THE INVASION OF EUROPE

(*U.S. Navy photograph*)

REAR-ADMIRAL JOHN L. HALL, U.S.N., ABOARD HIS FLAGSHIP, SERVING
WITH THE ALLIED NAVAL FORCES
(*U.S. Navy photograph*)

XII

THE NAVAL LEADERS

For their work continueth,
Broad and deep continueth,
Greater than their knowing.

RUDYARD KIPLING.

XII

THE NAVAL LEADERS

In what was once the library of an English country house, less than a dozen men gathered for a conference. They were in uniform because the library had become the Senior Officers' Mess of an all-important head-quarters. It was 4 A.M. and confirmation had to be given to a decision arrived at six hours earlier.

Presiding over the conference was General Eisenhower, Supreme Commander of the Allied Forces in the West. His companions were the Commanders-in-Chief of the three Services, their Chief of Staff and two or three members of General Eisenhower's personal staff.

Along the passage was the operations-room, with its huge map at one end and with strangely incongruous faded velvet pelmets over the French windows. Signals came in in a steady flow on an odd-looking conveyor, rather like the system used to send money to the cash-desk in a draper's shop. These signals, and the figures and entries written on a large board, were a constant reminder that the decision to be made involved the lives of literally hundreds of thousands of men.

No handful of men could have had a greater responsi-bility than those gathered in the Senior Officers' Mess. Twenty-four hours earlier they had been faced with exactly the same situation and had decided to postpone the great event for twenty-four hours.

They had arrived at that decision as the result of weather reports put before them by three weather experts, the senior of whom was a naval officer from Glasgow.

When that first decision was made it was a lovely calm night. Twenty-four hours later, when they gave confirmation to what had been agreed to at ten o'clock the previous evening—that the Invasion was " on "—

it was, in the words of an officer who was present, " blowing like the wrath of God."

The man who had the courage to commit an enormous naval force under these circumstances was Admiral Sir Bertram Home Ramsay, K.C.B., K.B.E., M.V.O., R.N., Allied Naval Commander of the Expeditionary Force. This supreme moment came to him at the age of sixty-one and after forty-five years in the Royal Navy.

In selecting high commanders it is easier, perhaps, to put the right man in the right job after five years of war rather than at the outbreak of hostilities. After five years there are the proven men to choose from ; nothing need be taken on trust. There is no doubt that Admiral Ramsay was the man to lead the Allied naval forces for the invasion of Europe. Behind the quick manner and twinkling brown eyes there is a brilliantly clear mind and a capacity for making rapid decisions, even when they are of the utmost importance.

It appeared that a long and distinguished service career had come to an end when Admiral Ramsay retired from the Navy at his own request in 1938. He had gone to his first ship, the *Crescent*, as a midshipman in 1899. Between that time and the outbreak of the last war he served in a number of ships, including the *Revenge*, *Terrible*, *Renown* and *Dreadnought*. In 1914 he was Flag Lieut.-Commander to Vice-Admiral Sir Douglas Gamble, commanding the 4th Battle Squadron. In 1915 he was given command of the Monitor M25 and spent some time off the Belgian coast. He became a commander in 1916 and a year later went to the Dover Patrol in command of the destroyer *Broke*, where he succeeded Admiral Sir Edward Evans, whose name will always be coupled with that of the famous destroyer.

Immediately after the war he was Flag Commander to Lord Jellicoe for a Dominions tour. Promoted to Captain in 1923, he commanded first the *Weymouth* and then the *Danae*, and in 1929, in the cruiser *Kent*, was Flag Captain and Chief of Staff to Vice-Admiral Waistell.

After a period on the staff of the Imperial Defence

College he was promoted to Flag rank and became Chief of Staff to Admiral Sir Roger Backhouse, in the Home Fleet.

Admiral Ramsay's retirement lasted only a few months, and then, with the outbreak of war, he became Flag Officer in Command, Dover. It was a return to the area he had known so well in the last war, but in a few months he was to be faced with a very different situation from any that had existed in the last war.

When the B.E.F. fought its way back to Dunkirk it devolved upon the Vice-Admiral, Dover, to plan and carry out the evacuation of the Army which was to become the main defence of these islands in the anxious months to come. If he had failed in this task the whole course of the war might have been changed.

Admiral Ramsay did not fail. With the help of such men as Admiral Sir James Somerville, another brilliant officer recalled from retirement, and a staff that was prepared to work night and day, he achieved a success that was beyond all expectations.

" Dynamo " was the code name for the Dunkirk evacuation, and as " Dynamo " Ramsay, the Admiral is known to the Navy to-day. Mobilising every ship and craft that could make the crossing to the Belgian coast, Admiral Ramsay brought out the B.E.F. from under the noses of the German army and, despite the worst the then powerful Luftwaffe could do.

At Dover at that time I watched the weary men of the B.E.F. disembark from every type of vessel. Many of them, almost too tired to stand, asked, " Is this England ? " and it must indeed have seemed a miracle to them that a bridge of ships had appeared from nowhere, as it were, to enable them to fall back on this country.

Admiral Ramsay was awarded the K.C.B. and the citation said : " For good services in organising the withdrawal to England, under fire and in the face of many and great difficulties, of 335,490 officers and men of the Allied Armies in about 1,000 of H.M. ships and other craft, between May 27th and June 4th, 1940."

Admiral Ramsay had handled his first armada, but it was a small and motley collection in comparison with the armada he was to control four years later.

After Dunkirk, Admiral Ramsay found himself with a command that was right in the front line. With the Germans twenty miles away, it became a matter of the greatest urgency to build up our defences in the south-eastern corner of England. He co-operated in this with the General Officer Commanding the South-Eastern Command—General Montgomery. He was also in close association with Air Vice-Marshal Sir Trafford Leigh-Mallory, who was at that time commanding No. 11 Group of the R.A.F. which was in the thick of the fighting over South-East England. Four years later these three commanders were to link together for the great invasion.

Admiral Ramsay made a special study of land operations and he was chosen to organise the planning of the Allies' first invasion on the grand scale—that of French North Africa. Admiral Sir Andrew Cunningham took supreme command of the expedition, which involved huge sea forces, and Admiral Ramsay served under him as Deputy Commander-in-Chief.

After the invasion had been successfully accomplished, an Allied communiqué stated that Admiral Ramsay's basic work, carried out in Britain pending the arrival of Admiral Cunningham from his post as head of the British Admiralty Delegation in Washington, " contributed in great measure to the excellent timing and smooth running of the convoy movements, which were of unprecedented complexity."

After North Africa, Admiral Ramsay worked on the plans for the invasion of Sicily, and, when the operation came about, took command at sea of the British forces. Having thus proved his special talent, it was only natural that he should be appointed, under General Eisenhower, who had been Supreme Commander of the Allied Expeditionary Force in North Africa, as Allied Naval Commander of the Expeditionary Force which was about to make the direct assault on Europe.

On D Day he commanded the greatest fleet, numerically, the world has ever seen ; 5,143 ships were concerned in the assault. The assault, however, was but the initial phase. Afterwards it was the naval forces under Admiral Ramsay that were responsibile for building up and maintaining the Allied armies on the Continent. In twenty-eight days from June 6th, 1944, more than a million fighting men were landed in France, with 183,500 vehicles and 650,000 tons of stores.

He had to meet the efforts of the enemy to interfere with this sea-line. There was the menace of mines, for instance, and in three months the total number of mines swept off the French coast represented ten per cent. of all the mines swept in five years of war, in all theatres of war.

There were other problems, such as " selective unloading " which appealed to the Army but had no virtues from the naval point of view. It meant that a number of ships would be held up at the landing points on the other side of the Channel, from which the Army could select what it desired to unload at any particular time. Admiral Ramsay, responsible for the quick turn round of vessels, set his face against the system, as he did against early suggestions that the convoy system might be relaxed. " I very often have to say ' No ' when it would be very pleasant to be able to say ' Yes,' " he remarked on one occasion. The Admiral's " No " is not to be argued with. It has also been of the greatest benefit to the Allied forces.

Admiral Ramsay has headed an Anglo-American team, as he himself is only too ready to say. The team has handled an enormous war organisation. In three months from D day over 100,000 signals passed through the Allied naval headquarters.

In the midst of his own manifold responsibilities, Admiral Ramsay has been quick to appreciate the work and needs of the other Services. In August, 1944, he wrote to Air Chief Marshal Sir Sholto Douglas, A.O.C.-in-C., R.A.F. Coastal Command : " Now that the Allied armies are firmly established in Normandy, and the initial stages of our operations may be said to have ended, the time seems appropriate to record my appreciation of the important part that Coastal Command has played throughout this period. The effectiveness of the anti-U-boat operations can be judged by their initial success in the north and south-western approaches, and the subsequent failure of the U-boat to achieve anything but the most meagre results within the Channel. Anti-shipping operations have been equally successful, and must have added a further unwelcome burden to the enemy's already overloaded transport system, while your aircraft so harried the enemy's coastal forces that they did not inflict the damage to our convoys which might otherwise have been expected. I would be grateful if the sense of this letter could be conveyed, with my congratulations and thanks, to the air and ground crews of all your squadrons, and those of the Allied nations and the Fleet Air Arm under your command, together with all others concerned in these most successful operations."

Admiral Ramsay was reinstated on the Active List in April, 1944, with the rank of Admiral.

Commanding the British Eastern Task Force for the invasion was Rear Admiral Sir Philip Louis Vian, K.C.B., K.B.E., D.S.O. and two bars, one of Britain's most famous wartime sailors. A gunnery specialist, he entered the Navy in 1907 and served all through the last war. He sprang into prominence in the early part of this war when he took the destroyer *Cossack* into Josing fjord and boarded the notorious German prison ship, *Altmark*. Three hundred seamen were rescued as a result of his daring. He commanded the *Afridi*, which was sunk in the evacuation of Mamsos, and showed fine leadership of the destroyers which harried the *Bismarck*.

He received his knighthood in 1941 for his brilliant work as commander of a squadron which got a convoy safely through to Malta in the face of heavy odds. Mr. Churchill subsequently described this as "a naval episode of the highest distinction."

Rear Admiral Vian commanded one of the three naval task forces under Admiral Ramsay for the invasion of Sicily. A man of forceful character, it is said that he knows no fear. His dashing leadership has become a by-word in the Navy. His sense of humour was expressed in a letter written to *The Times* newspaper in June, 1944, while he was still in the anchorage off the Normandy coast. It was as follows :

" SIR,—Look at the Derby and Oaks—

Derby :
Ocean Swell.—There was indeed.
Tehran.—Where it was all arranged.
Happy Landing.—It was.

Oaks :
Hycilla.

And I backed none of them !
                          Yours, PHILIP VIAN,
                                        Rear Admiral."
H.M.S. *Scylla*, June 19th.

Opposite number to Rear Admiral Vian was Rear Admiral Alan Goodrich Kirk, U.S.N., commanding the western naval Task Force. It was a happy selection that made Admiral Kirk the leading American naval figure for the Invasion. He has had much to do with the British Navy from the time he reported as Naval Attaché to the American Embassy in London in June, 1939. He was experienced, too, in landing operations, having commanded a naval task force alongside Admiral Ramsay for the landings in Sicily.

Born in Philadelphia, Pennsylvania, in 1888, he joined the U.S. Atlantic fleet as a Midshipman in 1909. Two years later he was in the U.S.S. *Wilmington* in the Far East and was at Canton during the Sun Yat Sen Revolution. As a Lieutenant he served in the Atlantic Fleet battleship *Utah* from 1914 to April, 1916, and then went to the

Naval Proving Ground, Dahlgren, Virginia, where he was in charge of the testing of the 14-inch guns which were subsequently fired from railway tracks in France. He became executive officer of the U.S.S. *Mayflower*, the Presidential yacht, with additional duty as Aide to the White House during several months of President Wilson's administration and during the first year of President Harding's.

Lieut. Commander Kirk was gunnery officer of the U.S.S. *Maryland* in 1925 and went with her on her goodwill cruise to Australia and New Zealand. Later he was given command of the destroyer *Schenck* and, in 1932, was executive officer of the U.S.S. *West Virginia*, flagship of Battleship Divisions, Battle Force.

After holding other important appointments, Rear Admiral Kirk came to London three months before the outbreak of the present war. He had many contacts with the Royal Navy and on the second day of the war flew to Galway, Ireland, to interview the Master and Officers of the S.S. *Athenia*. He made a report on the sinking of the vessel to President Roosevelt.

He returned to America towards the end of 1940 and it gave the utmost satisfaction in British naval circles when it was announced in March, 1942, that he had been appointed Chief of Staff and Aide to the Commander, U.S. Naval Forces in Europe, with additional duty as Naval Attaché at the American Embassy, London. After leading the Task Force in the Sicily landings, Rear Admiral Kirk received the Legion of Merit and the British Order of the Bath.

Rear Admiral John Lesslie Hall, U.S.N., and the late Rear Admiral Don Pardee Moon, U.S.N., were Commanders of units of Admiral Kirk's Task Force. They were both officers with outstanding service records and there was widespread regret when, in August, 1944, the Secretary of the Navy announced that Rear Admiral Moon had died. The official statement added, "Apparently Rear Admiral Moon had taken his own life as a result of combat fatigue."

Rear Admiral Moon, who was born in Kokomo, Indiana, in 1894, was a gunnery specialist. He commanded Destroyer Squadron 8 during the landings on the coast of French Morocco, in November, 1942, and received the commendation of the C.-in-C., Atlantic Fleet. Later his squadron served for an extended period with the British Home Fleet.

Rear Admiral Hall, a Virginian, had command of the U.S.S. *Arkansas* in 1940 and, a year later, became Staff Commander, Battleship Division 5. In September, 1942, he became Chief of Staff to the American Flag Officer with the British Fleet at Malta. Later he was appointed Commander of North African Sea Frontier forces and then Commander of a naval task force for the Sicily and Italy landings. During this war he has been awarded both the Distinguished Service Medal and the Legion of Merit.

Among the senior British naval officers commanding forces in the Eastern Task Force were Rear Admiral Arthur George Talbot, D.S.O., Rear Admiral William Edward Parry, C.B., Rear Admiral Cyril Eustace Douglas-Pennant, C.B.E., D.S.C., and Commodore Geoffrey Nigel Oliver, C.B., D.S.O. and bar.

Rear Admiral Talbot, who has commanded three famous aircraft carriers, the *Furious*, *Illustrious* and *Formidable*, during the war, was present at the Italy landings.

Rear Admiral Parry commanded the cruiser *Achilles* in the River Plate action with the *Graf Spee*. After a period as Chief of Naval Staff, New Zealand Naval Board, he returned and was given command of the battle cruiser *Renown*.

Rear Admiral Douglas-Pennant was with the Northern Patrol in the early part of the war. He was mentioned in despatches in 1943 for distinguished services in operations connected with the landing of Allied forces in North Africa.

Commodore Oliver joined the Navy with a special entry cadetship from Rugby during the last war. He served in the *Dreadnought* and *Renown*. In addition to the D.S.O. and bar awarded to him in this war, he received, in December, 1943, the Legion of Merit from the United States. The citation stated that it was for " exceptionally meritorious conduct of a high degree in the performance of outstanding services. A senior officer in charge of the inshore squadron operating in close support of the land force in the Tunisian campaign, Commodore Oliver's forces frequently provided needed support along the coast and were instrumental in intercepting enemy supplies. The activities of his force have aided greatly in bringing the Tunisian campaign to its successful climax." In May, 1944, he received the C.B. for gallantry and distinguished service in the planning and successful execution of the initial landings at Salerno.

Rear Admiral George Elvey Creasy, C.B., C.B.E., D.S.O., M.V.O., was a key man in the naval organisation required for the Invasion. As Chief of Staff to Admiral Ramsay, he was responsible for an enormous amount of the detailed work which enabled the whole gigantic operation to move smoothly forward when the moment to strike arrived. This was recognised by the award of the C.B. in July, 1944, for " distinguished services in the planning and execution of the successful Allied landings in Normandy." Before becoming Chief of Staff to Admiral Ramsay, Rear Admiral Creasy was in command of the battleship *Duke of York* and was Flag Captain to the C.-in-C., Home Fleet. In the early days of the war he was in command of the flotilla leader *Grenville*. When his ship was sunk in the North Sea in January, 1940, he swam about in the water leading his men in the singing of " Roll Out the Barrel."

Rear Admiral John Wilkes, U.S.N., was Commander of U.S. Landing Craft and Bases. He was in command of submarines which operated with outstanding success in Far Eastern areas during the campaign for the defence of the Philippine Islands and the Dutch East Indies, in 1941–42. The following year, in command of the U.S.S. *Birmingham*, he took part in the operations off Sicily.

He has been awarded both the Distinguished Service Medal and the Legion of Merit. Ensign John Wilkes, Jr., of the Naval Reserve, was on duty in the Pacific while his father led the way into Europe.

Commodore Campbell Dallas Edgar, U.S.N., Commander of the Follow-up forces, served in the last war in one of the American destroyers which operated out of Queenstown on Atlantic duties. He, too, received the Legion of Merit following the invasion of Sicily and for his part in the Italian invasion he received a Gold Star in lieu of a Second Legion of Merit. He was mentioned in British despatches for services at Algiers in 1942.

Here it is only possible to name a few of the naval commanders whose skill and courage had much to do with the success that crowned the greatest seaborne invasion in history. Those that I have mentioned would be the first to hand on their laurels to the hundreds of other officers whose devotion to duty lightened the burdens of the leaders.

*   *   *   *   *

It will be the historian who, in years to come, can make the final summing up ; this account, sketchy and incomplete as it is, may be of assistance as a documentary.

Nearly four months after D day, on September 28th, 1944, Mr. Churchill told the House of Commons, " The speed with which the mighty British and American armies were built up is almost incredible. In the first twenty-four hours, 250,000 men were landed in the teeth of fortified and violent opposition. By the twentieth day a million men were ashore. There are now between two and three million men in France. The progress in the power of moving troops and landing troops has vastly increased since the early days when we had to plunge into war with no previous experience. But the actual number of soldiers was only part of the problem of transportation. These armies were equipped with the most perfect modern weapons and every imaginable contrivance of modern war; an immense artillery supported all their operations and enormous masses of armour, of the highest quality and character, gave them extraordinary offensive power and mobility. Many hundreds of thousands of vehicles sustained their movement. Many millions of tons of stores have already been landed, and the great bulk of everything over open beaches or through the synthetic harbours. All this constitutes a feat of organisation and efficiency which should excite the wonder and deserve the admiration of all military students, as well as the applause of the British and American nations and their Allies."

The navies and merchant services were not specifically mentioned by Mr. Churchill but nobody would know better than he that the great bulk of these troops and supplies became effective only after they had taken passage in a British, American or Allied ship and had crossed the Channel with a safe escort provided by men-of-war.

And as the armies grew, the need for supplies increased accordingly. Fresh victories made new ports and landing areas available, but the first call was for the minesweepers to clear the way. Forty thousand Germans were still in Brest when I accompanied the first British minesweepers into the Morlaix river, not many miles away. Less than three weeks later, while I watched the Germans march out of their underground tunnels by the huge, empty U-boat pens, to surrender, Morlaix itself was taking in more than sufficient supplies for the fighting that remained to be done in the one or two ports still in German hands on the other side of the Brest peninsula.

Sandy bays that, in peace time, knew no more than a few colourful fishing craft, became alive with big Allied landing ships. Over the beaches, cleared of German obstructions, went the supplies for the armies. The L.S.T.'s came and went as if they were running on an endless belt.

And out in the wider seas, warships and aircraft swept

to and fro continuously to guard the link between England and France. The men in ships responded manfully to General Eisenhower's Order of the Day, issued in mid-August : " I request every sailor to make sure that no part of hostile forces can either escape or be reinforced by sea and that our comrades on the land want nothing that guns and ships and ships' companies can bring to them."

At every step the development of our offensive depended on ships—and more and more ships. For those who found themselves transporting supplies rather than engaging in the fighting there are the comforting words of Bernard Brodie, in his book " A Layman's Guide to Naval Strategy,"—" If the chief purpose of a navy is control of seaborne transportation, the vehicles of such transportation must be considered not as incidental to sea power but as an essential part of it. It would be as unreasoning to consider sea power in terms of warships alone as it would be to consider railroad trains in terms solely of locomotives. A locomotive without cars attached represents power well enough, but power without functional meaning."

Many are the lessons that will be learned from the great Invasion, but the one that stands clear above all others, is the continued need for free countries to control the seas. What Solikiowski said in the sixteenth century —" Who leaves the seas undefended and forsaken reaps no advantage but brings hardship upon himself. Free, he falls into slavery ; wealthy, he sinks into poverty "— remains true to-day.

And on the much debated question as to whether air power has changed, or will change, all this, I again quote Bernard Brodie : " Most of the materials that went into the construction of the British aircraft which hurled back the Luftwaffe in the Battle of Britain of 1940 and which took the offensive in 1942, were brought to the British Isles in ships. So, too, was all the fuel that those aircraft used, as well as most of the food that fed the men and women that made the planes, and the crews that flew them. The island base from which these aircraft operated would have been untenable without British command of the sea approaches from the west. It does not therefore detract in the least from the marvellous power of air forces to say that command of the sea is still as likely as formerly to be decisive in great wars, and that in fact the greatly increased quantity and complexity of the equipment used in modern war has made control of the sea lanes more important than ever before."

As the final chapter is being written in the comparatively narrow seas around the shores of these islands, we turn our eyes to the vast expanses of water which lie between us and our other enemy in the east. A large portion of " the fine modern British Fleet " is already gathered in the Indian Ocean. It will be employed in the major operations against Japan and will prove, in company with the enormously powerful Navy which has been built up by the United States, that sea power can lay the foundations of victory in two hemispheres.

THE END